OBJECTS OF
OUR AFFECTION

OBJECTS OF
OUR AFFECTION

.....

Uncovering my family's past,
one chair, pistol,
and pickle fork at a time

For Friends Select
with admiration

All best,
Lisa Tracy

LISA TRACY

SELECTED PHOTOGRAPHS BY
GINNY HILLHOUSE

BANTAM BOOKS

Copyright © 2010 by Lisa Tracy

Published in the United States by Bantam Books,
an imprint of The Random House Publishing Group,
a division of Random House, Inc., New York.

BANTAM BOOKS and the rooster colophon are
registered trademarks of Random House, Inc.

LIBRARY OF CONGRESS CATALOGING-IN-PUBLICATION DATA
Tracy, Lisa.
Objects of our affection : uncovering my family's past, one chair,
pistol, and pickle fork at a time / Lisa Tracy.
p.   cm.
ISBN 978-0-553-80726-4
eBook ISBN 978-0-553-90734-6
1. Tracy, Lisa—Family.   2. Personal belongings—Psychological
aspects.   3. Souvenirs (Keepsakes)—Psychological aspects.   4. House
furnishings—Psychological aspects.   5. United States—History,
Military—Miscellanea.   6. Families of military personnel—United
States—Biography.   I. Title.
CT275.T8217A3 2010
745.097309'04—dc22   2009047841

Printed in the United States of America

www.bantamdell.com

9 8 7 6 5 4 3 2 1

FIRST EDITION

Book design by Barbara M. Bachman

All my relations

Too much furniture in one's living room
Too many pens in a stand
Too many children in a house
Too many words when men meet
Too many books in a bookcase there can never be . . .

KENKO (FOURTEENTH CENTURY)

Not fare well,
But fare forward, voyagers.

T. S. ELIOT, *The Dry Salvages*

CONTENTS

PROLOGUE

I WAS IN THE OFFICE SUPPLY STORE TALKING TO BARbara, whom I've known since high school, and she asked what I was working on. Writing a book, I told her, about the family furniture. "Like family baggage," I said.

"Yeah, I know," said Barbara. "Only bigger."

We know, because this is who we are. We're Americans in the twenty-first century. We have more stuff in storage bins and basements and attics and back rooms than we can ever use in a lifetime. Or three.

And of all the things we probably should sort through and do something about, the family furniture is in a class by itself. Anytime I tell someone about my own family's voyage through the storage bins and on to the auction house and beyond, the story elicits winces of sympathy—and dread. If they haven't already wrestled with it, they know the time is coming.

The problem is compounded by the fact that we're living in the wealthiest country in the history of the world, and even as we know we should be winnowing, we are wallowing. It's hard to let go of objects because they are full of stories: our stories, our families' stories, or, if we've been haunting the flea market or the antiques mall, other people's stories. They speak to us, as Yeats once said, of what is past and passing and to come. They speak to us of the life we had, and lives we never knew.

I am sitting on a winter morning in the kitchen of a house my grandparents built. I'm eating breakfast with my great-nephew, and behind us on the counter is a plastic toy milk bottle that moos when you turn it upside down. His toy, from six or seven years ago. He's nine as I write. On this particular morning, I'm moved to suggest that we might get rid of it. Pass it on to someone else, someone younger, perhaps? *Yes*, he says unthinkingly, then immediately reneges.

The milk bottle, he tells me, reminds him of when he and his dad were living in the country. One night, his dad was making popcorn in a skillet, and when he took it off the stove and opened the lid, the fluffed kernels exploded all over the place. "And when the popcorn blew up, I was looking at the milk bottle, and it put the remembering right in my head," he explains. The memory still makes him laugh uproariously. And this is why, I see, we won't be getting rid of this milk bottle anytime soon.

We can, in fact, never be free of our stuff until we have dealt with the stories it carries. In the end, it does indeed tell us something about who we are. It's just stuff, our possessions. Family furniture. And it's what we make of it.

OBJECTS OF
OUR AFFECTION

Chapter 1

THE
BEGINNING

THE DAY WE PACKED THE HOUSE, I WAS IN THE LIVING ROOM
sorting family pictures and papers when the movers came.
One mover, to be precise: He was the advance guard, the packing man.

It was a beautiful October day in 1992, still warm but with
an edge in the air. Fall had come to the mountains around the
small Virginia town where I'd grown up, but the flame-colored
ridges weren't what I'd come for. I was wrestling with the contents of a chest of drawers where my mother had deposited a
pile of family papers. There were genealogy charts, military
commendations, fragments of biographies, letters from the
War of 1812, a photocopy of a journal dating from the 1840s,
and what seemed like dozens of little framed daguerreotypes of
people whose identity was a complete mystery to me. All had
to be sorted and packed, because when my sister, Jeanne, came
later that week, we'd be helping our eighty-three-year-old
mother move—not particularly willingly—to a retirement

home from the house she'd occupied for forty years. It had been her parents' house, then hers and Daddy's.

She had been living alone for almost twenty-five years now, and people had recently started calling us with worrisome anecdotes and dire predictions, all of course veiled in polite concern, this being a small town where certain formalities still obtained. She was making unexplained withdrawals from her bank account. She would walk aimlessly, turning up at the church at unexpected times. Her driving was atrocious, had been for years.

Mother had told us herself that she really didn't think she should be living alone, and for a while my nephew had lived at the house with her. We'd looked for live-in help without much success. There weren't many options. I'd found only one candidate, a woman who didn't drive and who smoked. We're a small family, just Jeanne and me in our generation, and we were both living hundreds of miles away. What were we to do?

The only retirement home—we didn't want a nursing home, just someplace safe where she would have help—was the old hotel, a relic of an earlier time, as the worn carpet and small, rather dark rooms reminded us when I went with her to look at it. She agreed to the corner room overlooking the street all too close to our house—her house—just a quick walk down to the corner, across the street, and down the alley. Acceded with teeth clenched, a gracious face, and the steely determination to fight again as soon as the opponent's back was turned. We thought she was adjusting remarkably well to the inevitable. She fooled us.

The men of the family—on both sides, Mother's and Daddy's—had been high-ranking military officers, their wives gracious hostesses. The accumulated social power of that household, reflected in all its furnishings and memorabilia, made moving out quite a comedown. For Mother, leaving all that gentility behind must have seemed like an admission of weakness, a failure, a defeat. She was abandoning ship, and I think it broke her heart. But, as was typical of our true-blue military family with its Victorian ways, she didn't say, and we didn't ask, how she felt about it. She put on her stiffest upper lip and moved.

She would be dead within six months. But we didn't know that then, of course. On this mid-October day, the move and all that would follow were still ahead of us, and I was on an archaeological dig, plowing through layers of family possessions we'd managed to ignore for decades, or in some cases had never seen before. And that's when the man we would come to know as Roger arrived.

"Where would you like me to start?" he asked, surveying the living room I'd strewn with papers. *Not here*, I thought. The last thing I needed in the living room at this point was helping hands. I took him to the dining room and showed him the contents of the Hepplewhite cabinet that we used as a china closet, which I figured would keep him busy for a while, even with his fancy shrink-wrap.

But in less than an hour, he was back. "I'm finished with the china," he said, looking pretty pleased with himself. "What would you like me to do next?"

I was still excavating the bowfront chest of drawers— a homely thing with an ashen-colored veneer and drawers that tended to jam. I was also probably irritated that this guy was interrupting me again already; I was on a short leash, with a demanding job and a preteen son six hours up the East Coast, and I had just a few days here to get as much packed as possible.

Mother—who was in no real hurry to move anywhere—wasn't helping. Now it was dawning on me that movers required supervision. What, they didn't come with a floor plan of your house and telepathic powers?

I took Roger to the kitchen and opened the cabinets where the daily china lived: parts of a set of Noritake, badly faded from the dishwasher; all the glassware; the Italian faience creamers and sugar bowls; the remnants of blue-and-white Canton my grandmother had used for breakfast dishes, and we after her; the tea sets and coffee cups.

He looked a little crestfallen, but rallied and got on with some more shrink-wrapping. After about another hour, he reemerged, grim but triumphant. "All right," he said evenly. "I'm done with the china. What's next?"

Here he was again. I really wanted to get all these papers into a box I would recognize next time I saw it—in the storage bin or wherever—in case we needed it in a hurry. And I wanted to get it done before Mother came back from whatever errand she'd gone out on, so we wouldn't have to discuss the whole business: the unwelcome move and the odious packing, much less the papers and photos and all the family history they might represent, which we definitely didn't have time to go into right now. Yes, Roger would have to be kept occupied until I'd at least dispatched the contents of these drawers.

I led him to the basement, to the walk-in closet that had held my grandmother's preserves. Now it was a repository for Christmas decorations, broken lamps, bric-a-brac, and glassware. In the middle of the center shelves stood stacks of plates. One hundred thirty rose medallion Canton luncheon plates, to be exact. I gestured to them apologetically. Roger shot me a dirty look.

One drawer yielded a jumble of wills, journals, family trees, photos, newspaper clippings, and military documents.

"Right," he muttered. I left him there and went back to the papers in the living room. If he thought we had a lot of stuff, well, he'd only had to deal so far with the china. It was quite a while before I saw him again, but meanwhile I had begun to wonder. Granted, our family had quite an assortment of china, from years, I supposed, of entertaining, to say nothing of inheriting from forebears. But what exactly were we doing with a hundred-some luncheon plates of any kind, much less Canton?

Chapter 2

THE CANTON PLATES

THE CHINA, AS MUCH AS ANYTHING, EXEMPLIFIES THE DIF-
ficulty of dismissing the family furniture—or trying to. For
me, it represents my grandmother Bess, the woman we called
Granny.

Elizabeth "Bess" Egbert was born in 1872 into an Army
family stationed at a remote outpost in California. Camp
Independence, in Paiute territory at the foot of the Sierra
Nevada, was far from the civilized world. In 1872, Thomas
Edison had just earned $40,000—an astonishing sum—for
improvements to the stock market's ticker and was establishing
his first real laboratory. A confederation of German states had
stunned the world by trouncing France and invading Paris. But
here in the Owens Valley of California's high desert country,
the earthshaking event was an 8.1 quake that tore a rift in the
valley floor. Amazingly, it killed only a handful of people at
the one settlement of any note in the area, Lone Pine, where
they died in their beds under falling adobe bricks.

At Camp Independence, an Army post just up the road

from Lone Pine, Capt. Harry Egbert and his wife, Nelly, were among those who shook in their beds that night but lived to tell the tale of how they'd escaped the quake. Nine months later, a few days after Christmas of that year, little Elizabeth—Bess, or Bessie, as they would call her—was born, the Egberts' second child and their first daughter.

Bess would have little memory of the post or of the towering Sierra Nevada that loomed in the near distance. By the time she was six, her father had been transferred through at least seven assignments, including a trip to Washington escorting what his service papers describe simply as "an insane soldier," and campaigns in Indian territory in Idaho. For longer postings, the family typically moved with him. It was probably with some road-weariness, then, that they arrived at Fort Verde, near the rich bottomland of Arizona's aptly named Verde River. It was 1878, just before Bess's sixth birthday. They might well have taken a steamboat up the Colorado River as far as Fort Yuma, a route favored by the Army. Nelly later recounted how they left Fort Yuma to cross the forbidding Mojave Desert through Apache territory in Army ambulances—covered wagons with benches in the back that could convert into bunks—carrying all of their drinking water with them. They stayed for a full four years in Arizona, where Bess's father—a Civil War veteran, and by now one of the Army's more senior line officers—at one point served a term as the territory's judge advocate.

In the course of dealing with the furniture after Mother died, I'd started looking for information to better understand who this woman, my grandmother, was. And when I did, I found Harry Egbert on the Web. Harry, it turned out, had led a sufficiently flamboyant life to show up more than once. The

Egberts, moreover, had lived in times and places that went down in history for other reasons. More Web searches turned up not only Camp Independence but also Fort Verde. Fort Verde, I found, had a website: The fort had become an Arizona state historic park and museum, "the best preserved example of an Indian Wars period fort in Arizona." In the heart of Apache territory, it was also, I learned, the primary base for scouts reporting to George Crook, the U.S. Army general who helped bring about the surrender and exile of the legendary Apache warrior Geronimo.

The day I stumbled on the Forte Verde website, I picked up the phone—why not?—and was soon talking with a staff curator at the fort, located somewhere in the foothills north of Phoenix. It was a slow day in the park, and she was happy to look for the Egberts in the museum files. It would have been in April of the year the Egberts arrived there, she mentioned in passing, that Geronimo had left the San Carlos reservation to the east of Fort Verde, passing within miles of the fort as he successfully evaded the U.S. Cavalry and fled south.

"Oh, this is interesting," she said, moments later. "There's a whole series of letters here—it looks like a real squabble!" It seemed that Captain Egbert, who was serving as Fort Verde's commanding officer, had been accused by a junior officer of hogging the best house on the post. The Army, precise in its allotments, had prescribed three rooms for a commanding officer with family , and the Egberts had taken possession of their allotted space in the large adobe bungalow, while this lieutenant had a fourth room. They shared a common living and dining room and the kitchen. Although the lieutenant was surely an unsought-for boarder in the Egbert household (where the U.S. government was of course the undisputed landlord), they seem to have started out amicably enough. The trouble began when the lieutenant married and applied for an additional room. As things progressed, it appears tempers rose, and Lieutenant West and

*Harry and
Nelly Egbert*

Captain Egbert sent a series of increasingly huffy letters via mail pouch to Army regional headquarters. And as the Army took its time to ponder their arguments—eventually denying the lieutenant his application—you can just imagine the two couples and the Egberts' children crowding the common room of an evening: the children roughhousing, the officers gritting their teeth and trying to get some paperwork done, the wives—strangers, really—straining to make polite conversation over their mending, about the difficulty of getting the enlisted men to bring in the firewood, perhaps, or the surliness of the company's laundresses. In front of the children, they'd likely have kept to themselves their thoughts about the remaining Apaches who might still be lurking in the foothills across the arroyo.

Rummaging in the park files, the curator also dredged up pictures of typical homes from isolated Army posts in the late 1880s, including interior photos that showed what she described as "a remarkable abundance of stuff "—all sorts of ornaments and small household objects that an officer's family hauled with them to define their quarters as home wherever they traveled. Army families were allowed a certain number of pounds of household belongings, depending on rank and expected duration of stay. An officer of Harry Egbert's rank would have had something like a one-thousand-pound allotment, and the Army Quartermaster Corps would have taken care of moving it by train and then wagon to the family's new home in Fort Verde. Typically that thousand pounds would include clothing, personal effects, status symbols such as portraits and the good tableware, and a few precious pieces of decent furniture.

When officers and their families arrived at frontier posts like Fort Verde, the curator noted, they would cobble together a décor made up of their own possessions and whatever they could buy from those who were departing. A nineteenth-century manual at Fort Verde shows how to construct tables and chairs from packing boxes, just one indication of how strapped Army families were for furnishings, thousands of miles from anything resembling a department store. That, the curator said, explained the abundance of throws in photos from the museum's archives. Easily packed squares of colorful fabric, woven or knitted, they could mask a dilapidated chair or settee or cover a scarred table while providing the comfort of familiarity as their owners moved from place to place.

The Canton china was still decades in the family's future at this point, but Army records tell us that even on the frontier, on the edge of Indian territory with scorpions and centipedes, 110-degree summers and freezing winters, the typical Army wife brought as much as she could carry of her silver, linens, china, and bric-a-brac. She had a position to maintain, appearances to keep up. She would, after all, have to marshal her forces on the only front available to a nineteenth-century Army wife, that of her husband's advancement.

In this setting, it's not too much of a leap to think that the chair we called the Egbert rocker, which always held the place of honor next to my grandparents' fireplace, might have been part of the baggage that traveled with Harry and Nelly to Fort Verde. It wasn't heavy; it wouldn't have taken up that much of their total allotment, and it would definitely make a place feel more like home. A curiously carved piece of Victoriana, it came down to us covered in velvet, though it might well originally have been leather. It was one of the chairs the men of the family sat in, prompting the thought that it might have been Harry's favorite, the refuge he'd sink into upon his return to their Fort Verde quarters after a few days' reconnoitering with his men out in the dust and sagebrush.

Over the next decade, the Egbert family dutifully packed up the silver, the linens, the knickknacks, the necessary range of clothing for summer deserts and winter mountains, and perhaps the cherished chair and another larger piece or two, then unpacked and packed it all again as they moved from post to post, sometimes for a year or two, sometimes for only a few months. On one such move to Wyoming, they stayed through December 1890 and January 1891 while Harry Egbert led his men to a place in South Dakota called Wounded Knee, where part of his infantry regiment was called to back up the Seventh Cavalry during its infamous raid on the Lakota Sioux.

Through all their moves, an officer's daughter's chief obligations were constant: learn housekeeping and basic schoolroom skills; be charming, hospitable, and demure; and be ready, when the time came, to marry a suitable officer. By now the Egbert family included three girls, and as Bess and her sisters grew toward adulthood, their mother must have kept an eye out for suitors along the family's whirlwind trail. Not for her daughters the conventional rituals of Eastern debutantes. They would have to seek their marital fortunes on these isolated posts. The odds were in their favor, by the numbers: about forty men for every woman on a typical post in the Western states. But of those, only perhaps half a dozen would be officers; and of course an enlisted man wouldn't do.

For Bess, there was an additional obstacle. Sometime during her childhood, she had fallen and cut her face. It was a disfiguring injury that severed the nerves in her left cheek above the mouth, causing her whole visage to skew to that side. The scars would ultimately cost her the suitor of her choice, who courted her and then broke off the engagement to marry, as she would later recount the story, a prettier woman.

When Bess did finally marry in the spring of 1900, she was all but past the age, by Victorian standards, to make a good catch. She and my grandfather met and courted in the midst of three consecutive wars, which first carried both of them to the

Philippines, and soon took her new bridegroom, young Lt. Charles Kilbourne, off to China, where American troops were dispatched to lift the "siege of the legations" during the Boxer Rebellion.

Bess was pregnant seven times. My mother—also Elizabeth, nicknamed Betty—was the only child who lived to adulthood. One daughter died at birth. There were miscarriages. And there was Carlos, their first son.

Carlos. I see my grandparents, in a moment of exhilaration at the birth of this boy who would carry on the line, naming him Charles, after my grandfather, but dubbing him Carlos in a lighthearted nod to the islands where they had met and married and where their son was born. Carlos, son of a man who had helped to win those islands from Spain and then subdue the Filipino rebels—a man who, according to newspaper accounts of the time, had played a gallant role in that campaign. Although they wouldn't have seen it that way, Charles and Bess were part of the advance guard of their country's fledgling imperialism. Awash in the exuberance of their youth, they stood at the dawning of the American century, adventurous, proud, triumphant. But they had no power over death, and Carlos would be one of their terrible losses.

Carlos died on board the ship that carried the family home in 1911 to the States from the Philippines, where his younger sister, Betty, had been born as well. He was seven or eight at the time. She was two years old, and probably longing for the Filipino nursemaid, her "ayah," left behind.

Carlos, as Mother told me more than once, was just one of many children stricken with amebic dysentery aboard the vessel, a ship of death for the frantic families for whom there was no escape. The distraught parents, she said grimly, watched as

Carlos with his ayah

their children's bodies were given sea burial. In her remembrance, she was the only child to live. This couldn't be so, I think now; of course she didn't really remember it, how could she? And yet she spoke as if she did. She was telling us what must have been her parents' memory, but it became her reality. "They all died," she would say, gazing accusingly into the past. "And they threw them overboard."

Mother's life, for certain, would never be the same. Survivor's guilt had not yet been named, but it was part of her. She raced ahead in school, moving to a new Army post or city as often as once a year, graduating from a private girls' school at age fourteen. She smiled engagingly for the camera and crossed her ankles demurely. And she inwardly cursed the fate that had left to her parents not the firstborn son, but the shy, slightly bucktoothed daughter.

Another child, born after my mother, survived into his teens. He was known to us only as Little Brother, for she never referred to him any other way, when she referred to him at all. Born with Down syndrome, he was accorded affection but, in the manner chronicled by Faulkner in *The Sound and the Fury*, never called by his given name. Among the family photos, there is a picture of a dark-haired, stolid child sitting on the steps of one of their many Army quarters. Is it Little Brother? And what would they have called him, if they had called him by name? It was only after Mother's death, when I visited the grave in Arlington where he and my grandparents are buried, that I learned that he too, futilely, bore the name Charles, after his father.

Years after my sister and I are grown and gone from home—sometime in the 1980s, I think—I'm back for a visit. Mother, now a widow, lives alone in the house that had originally been our grandparents'. She enters a room and half-irritably asks me to turn off a jazz recording on the stereo. *You don't really like music,* I say, surprised at the sudden recognition of the fact. *Why?*

Because, she says, *it was one of the ways I used to keep Little Brother amused.* She has that pained look I know so well, the same look she's worn on those occasions when she has tried to deal with us, her children, in emotional or physical distress. She reaches out and shrinks back at the same time, in a dichotomy of duty and discomfort. *I used to play the phonograph for hours,* she says.

I turn the stereo off and we change the subject.

The cost of it all to my grandmother was never reckoned. The disfigured face. The surgery to mend it. The scars, the jilting. And finally the lost children. Her patient, intelligent profile was almost always captured in formal photos from the good side. She smiled stoically when caught full face in candid shots.

It was she who taught me to say "please" and "thank you" and of course "yes, ma'am." (Me from the bottom of the stairs, circa age four, in answer to a question from above: "Yesss!" My grandmother, unseen but imperious from beyond the head of the stairs: "Yes, *what?*" Me, meekly from below: "Yes, ma'am.") As an Army child and the wife of an officer, Bess lived in quarters ranging from cramped to elegant, but never in a house of her own until she was nearly seventy. Two Yankee wanderers, she and my grandfather finally settled in Lexington, Virginia. Though named for the Revolutionary War's opening battle in Lexington, Massachusetts, it was a town where the exploits of Stonewall Jackson and Robert E. Lee were much more vividly remembered. My grandfather, son of a Union officer, had been sent to this Southern town as a young man in the 1890s, to attend Virginia Military Institute.

He came back to Lexington almost fifty years later, after a life-time in the Army, to serve as the institute's superintendent throughout yet another war. When he retired in 1946, he and Bess moved to the house they'd built at the edge of town, and he laid out a garden in the backyard for her roses, the American Beauties and Dainty Besses that would grace her table in a Chinese bowl.

While my grandparents were finally—for the first time in their lives, both having spent their entire lives on Army posts—living in their own house, and a pretty nice one at that, my parents, my sister, and I were a mere two blocks away, in-habiting what felt like an entirely different universe. For us, the post–World War II housing shortage translated into a rented house with an assertive clan of rats and a refrigerator made from an old icebox.

On days when I walked those two long blocks to visit, I'd likely arrive to find my grandmother having someone to tea. As befitted children in her still-Victorian world, I would be pleas-antly but irrefutably banished from the adults' company, down the narrow hallway past the Chinese screen to her and my grandfather's bedroom. Would I like to play with the jewelry box while the grown-ups visited? She knew, of course. It was our pact, and when she left me there alone, it was our silent but continuing mode of communication, this padded silk Chinese box with its removable tray and its many little compartments and drawers and the blue and scarlet dragons on its lid. She'd pull a chair up to the low dresser and there I'd sit dreamily until dinnertime, arranging and rearranging the pearl and jade pins, the mismatched beaded earrings, the rhinestone necklaces, drift-ing in a matrix of fantasy woven from the box and from the pages of a storybook she'd bought me, with exquisite illustrations of Aladdin in a garden of jewels, its bushes bending under sprays of amethyst and tourmaline and lapis.

She brought to that house an array of objects gathered from four continents. The Canton china was among them.

The rose medallion Canton tea set traditionally traveled in its own padded basket.

THE CANTON CHINA. Most of it was "rose medallion," porcelain that by the second half of the nineteenth century was more or less mass-produced in the Chinese province of Kwantung.

There were dinner plates, butter plates, coffee cups and saucers, dessert plates, teacups and consommé cups, and a three-quart punch bowl that for most of our lives simply sat on the sideboard, gathering Christmas cards once a year.

As a child I was as fascinated by the Canton china as by her jewelry box. To look at the intricate scenes painted on the sides of the plates and bowls was to step inside Aladdin's world. Ladies and courtiers, merchants and scholars went about their business there, framed in flower-edged panels with fine black lines defining every detail. A kaleidoscopic life spoke through the panels—foreign faces, exotic garments, a mysterious swirl of activity captured in stillness and silence. The translucent porcelain whose formula of clay and metals took the Europeans centuries to replicate emanated in the 1700s and 1800s from the port Westerners called Canton. The Chinese had been making it for several centuries at that point, but when they realized the extent of their market, they speeded up and expanded the process. The delicate ware was fired at inland kilns, painted in the city's workshops, and shipped abroad from the port. The hongs, or merchant families, had a monopoly on exports and controlled the price, taking their cut from the China trade.

By the mid-nineteenth century, the distinctive early cobalt-and-white Canton and the finely glazed *famille verte* and *famille rose* porcelain had given way to the bolder, heavier greens, rose, black, and gilt of the rose medallion ware. The demand was such that pattern chests—a precursor of the catalog—were sent abroad, and Cantonese workshops had assembly lines of workers each specializing in one or more details of the design.

The Canton was but one of my grandmother's sets of good china; what shoes were to other women, china may well have been to Bessie. There were also the Minton, the Doulton, the Worcester, the Wedgwood, and the Staffordshire. But the Canton was the most extensive.

The luncheon plates, I reckon, had a distinct role to play in all of this. As an officer's wife, Bess Kilbourne would have entertained. Among the wives' duties in the myriad unlikely places where they found themselves was to organize endless musical soirées, readings, charades, amateur theatricals, and dances. Perhaps once a year, a ranking officer and his wife would feel obligated to invite everyone of any note—officers, local dignitaries, visitors, their families; you'd be lucky if you ended up with only a hundred people. A dinner would have been prohibitively expensive—all those courses, on an officer's salary, to say nothing of the alcohol, with the attendant risk of people lingering for hours and consuming a perhaps unseemly amount. A luncheon, however, could be safely contained. Elegant little portions of this and that, some fruit and pastries . . . a punch, perhaps, with the assurance that all the guests would be gone by midafternoon and you'd have the rest of the day to deal with the wreckage. And that, after all, would be minimal, since the drinking set would have repaired to the officers' club instead of your living room to continue their revels.

If the occasional Canton plate did get broken, it didn't matter. This china, our mother told us, was virtually the paper plate of its day in the Philippines, where they'd obtained it—at ten cents a plate, the cheapest thing you could buy, and if a few plates or even a few dozen were broken, no great loss. Always more where that came from.

And so the one hundred thirty plates. There probably were more. Who knows. Whether the disposable Canton or a valuable heirloom, one's china was a measure of the gracious life—the elegantly set table, with immaculate linen and glistening silver and crystal. Throughout her many moves, her unrelenting travels, Army histories tell us, an officer's wife packed the china, hoping to see it arrive more or less intact at its next destination—God and the Quartermaster Corps willing—to properly impress whatever fellow officers' wives she'd be dealing with at the next outpost. There was stability and strength in the china, a paradox.

For me, though, thinking of my grandmother Bess, the Canton china has another resonance. Bess had her wounds—that face always turned aside, the sting of being jilted, the indignity of being merely a woman in a man's world—and she had her casualties: of seven pregnancies, only one child left among the living. Three not to be at all, the miscarriages. Of the other three dead, Carlos and their first daughter, stillborn in the Philippines, were not even buried where she might visit them; the third, their Down syndrome brother, doomed to a short life. Nothing you could do to make it better except to love him while he lived. The china, for all its fragility, survived them. For people, even those closest to her, my grandmother evinced a quiet aloofness. You loved the people. The objects, sadly, were more durable. And in the officer corps, where competition for promotion was intense, life did not stop for people. Life went on.

Bess Kilbourne was the daughter of one distinguished officer and the wife of another, surrounded from birth by what Stephen Covey would call Highly Effective People. Bess, though properly brought up to be decorous, a gracious hostess and good listener, was no less determined. Her composure masked a strong will, and in my childhood memories of her house, that will revealed itself not only in her formidable personal presence, but in the most minute details of the housekeeping.

By the time we knew her, she had it down to a science. Her household was probably more organized than the Quartermaster's storehouse. She knew what she needed to make people feel comfortable, welcome, and well entertained, and she marshaled the requisite resources: good linens, wool blankets, down comforters. A pitcher of water and clean glasses in every guest room. A linen closet with a shelf of household remedies in case of headache or dyspepsia, cuts or bruises. A drawer for candles and another for cocktail napkins. A chiffonier full of sewing supplies. A pantry with a walk-in china closet. Bells in three downstairs rooms to summon a servant from the kitchen, with numbers on the kitchen buzzer to indicate which room; demitasse and liqueurs by the fireplace in winter, iced drinks on the terrace in summer.

The blankets, comforters, towels, pitchers, and glasses were color coded for each guest room, so that neither guests nor family would have to wonder which washcloth or water glass was theirs; and I am sure that if patterned sheets had been thought of, she would have had them. Leafing through a *New York Times* home and design section, I come across an article on the influential early twentieth-century interior decorator Dorothy Draper. In the footnotes I recognize a picture of the green, white, and rose pattern that went to make up the summer slipcovers in our living room. Of those very slipcovers, my grandmother famously remarked—upon a visit from evangelist Pat Robertson's mother, who lived down the block—"Well, if Gladys is so sure about when the world is coming to an end, I wish she would tell me, so I'd know whether I should bother to get out the summer things."

It was a far cry from the hodgepodge furniture of the frontier.

Chapter 3

AT THE BINS

WE GREW UP WITH THE FURNITURE, MY SISTER AND I, in the household that was our grandmother Bess's creation. When she died in the early 1950s, Jeanne was in middle school and I had just completed first grade. Before school started again two months later, we'd moved from our rented house to live with her recently widowed husband, our grandfather Charlie.

Mother said he shouldn't live alone. He had been completely devoted to the wife whose table he furnished with the roses that bore her name, and it was hard to imagine him there without her in the house they had built together just ten years earlier. But the move to the brick house on Pendleton Place was definitely a step up in the world for us; even a child could see that.

The brick house was also home to what we'd come to think of as *the* furniture—not Daddy's comfortable old wingback chair, or the somewhat threadbare sofa in the living room of our rented house, where the feisty rats one night found straw coasters that had been left out and chewed them to pieces under the dining room table. At our grandparents', there were actual antiques. We didn't really know about antiques. We just knew that this was a lot of very old stuff that the grown-ups obviously thought was very important, and it came with rules attached. There was the George Washington chair, as it had always been called, for instance. An armchair upholstered with flocked dull fabric, it always sat under the front window in Bessie and Charlie's living room. We'd been instructed since early childhood in the doctrine of its delicacy. When a certain very stout neighbor was seen in full sail on the sidewalk, obviously about to pay a call, one of the grown-ups would summon whichever of us was more readily available to occupy the George Washington chair until Mrs. Q. was safely seated in another.

The Chinese wedding lamps were in the same class as the Washington chair. Time out of mind they had sat high on a mantel or atop the china cabinet, safely out of range, and we were warned never under any circumstances to touch them. As if. And God forbid a stray beanbag should ever come near them, as happened that night in 1954 when we inadvertently smashed the magenta Christmas ornament while playing too near the tree. I caught hell for that one.

❧

IT WOULD BE ALMOST a full ten years after Mother died before we'd ask ourselves just what we were planning to do with it all. That October, as we did our packing and directed the movers, we saw the bins as a stopgap measure, Jeanne and I. We were just flying by the seat of our pants, driven by a sense of urgency to get Mother settled someplace where she'd be looked after. We'd found her the room at the retirement home. The house obviously couldn't sit empty indefinitely, but we hadn't decided what to do about it just yet.

We considered the retirement home a stopgap solution too. It didn't have to be permanent. People in our small town of Lexington had all kinds of arrangements for elder care, from three-generation households to live-in help. Perhaps in a few months we could find someone to live with her at home, at 1 Pendleton Place. Maybe Mother would come to live with one of us and we'd rent the house. We hadn't found the ideal solution yet, but for now she was safe. And for now, we'd put the furniture in storage, where it too would be safe.

For about a month, the house was simply locked, those two short blocks from her new, so inadequate abode, while we waited for the movers to work our bigger pieces—the stuff that hadn't gone with Roger that first day—into their schedule. I suddenly imagine how she must have disdained our seemingly temporary and shortsighted transgression, quietly leaving the retirement home and walking to her real home, the house, with a key she'd surely have had—to let herself in and sit, perhaps enjoying a little wine or bourbon, plotting her return as soon as she'd brought us to our senses.

Then we swept back to finish emptying the house, still oblivious to her anguish. There wasn't much time to thrash through it all, to triage and pack a half dozen or so lifetimes' worth of stuff before the movers came to escort the big pieces, including the sofa, to storage.

And so we joined the ranks of the estimated one in ten American households that the Self Storage Association, a trade organization, reports spent more than $20 billion in 2008 to store—what? Precious valuables? Junk? Really useful stuff?

Or all those things that, frankly, we just haven't wanted to think about until, well, later?

When Roger arrived at our house that October day, I'm sure he thought he'd simply come to help us pack. But he set in motion a whole other process with his innocently fateful question: *Where do you want me to start?*

Where do you want me to start? Oh, yes. Where does any of us start? For Roger, the question was simply a practical point of departure. For us—the packees, if you will, or more truthfully, the pack*rats*—the movers and their trucks and storage bins were testament to the fact that we hadn't started. We hadn't begun to deal with the real problem: not packing the furniture, but unpacking all that was inside it.

※|※

ROGER HAD TAKEN ALL the china that day and the pictures and paintings, things that had to be wrapped and handled carefully. I'd packed bags of old clothes and costume jewelry for the thrift shop, and emptied all the drawers of the bowfront chest of drawers and the dining room drawers full of linen and silver and the bureau that had all the checkbooks and old Christmas cards and stuff, and I'd boxed the towels and sheets from the linen closet and thrown out the almost-empty bottles of hydrogen peroxide and calamine lotion and out-of-date cough syrup. That was pretty much it for the downstairs. Then Jeanne had arrived and we'd taken Mother to her new abode. Afterward I'd fled back to New Jersey, leaving to Jeanne and her son—my nephew, David—the task of clearing out the upstairs, with the unsorted remnants of our childhoods still in the closets and several hundred pounds of books on their shelves in various bedrooms.

When we went back to our respective homes, it was with a sense of relief. Mother was in good health, if not entirely in good spirits at this upheaval we'd foisted on her. We were sure she'd adjust. After all, she did have the corner room, looking out toward the mountains; that was something. (Already the retirement home wasn't looking so bad to us. After all, we weren't the ones living there.) And we'd see about moving her to a second floor room, with a better view, when one opened up. A room with a view, a real view—who could ask for anything more?

But it didn't work out that way. We moved her in October. In March, she tripped and fell crossing the threshold into a friend's house. A threshold, not even a stairway or a curb. She went to the hospital with a broken hip, caught pneumonia, and within three weeks was dead. It was the same way her father, our grandfather Charlie, had died. The hip, the infection, the infirmity of age; there was a certain déjà vu, almost an inevitability about it, for both of us, Jeanne and me. We busied ourselves with the details of a memorial service and cleaning out the room at the retirement home. We carried her up to West Point to be buried beside Daddy, a trip that recalled a bleak day twenty years earlier, when she and Jeanne and I— just the three of us, on a cold winter morning—had traveled there with the urn that contained his ashes.

There was a finality in Mother's death; both she and Daddy had been their parents' only surviving child, and she was the last of them, of our immediate family. Now it was just Jeanne and me, Jeanne's son, David, and my son, Owen.

Of course we were still in denial at that point. But we were used to being alone. We'd been used to long distances, and to polite inconsequential conversation at the dinner table when we were together. I would sometimes think of the scene in *Annie Hall* where the screen splits and you see the big Jewish family arguing and laughing at dinner on one side, and the prim Norman Rockwell family on the other. We were the Norman Rockwell version, and the absence of even those who are present was nothing new. This departure was just more of the same, the conclusion of a long process. We were a military family first and foremost, and so perhaps we'd been in some kind of denial for a long time. And denial was particularly convenient at this point, since it allowed us to get back home to our lives, our jobs, our families. It all seemed nicely final.

The years after Mother's death were the span that saw my son, Owen, grow up from Little League and G.I. Joes, ice hockey and art classes, to middle-school dances, first-year Spanish, and playing Black Sabbath covers in a rock band. He'd learn to drive a stick shift; he'd take pre-calc and attend the prom. In those same years, my nephew would come live with us for a summer in an old frame twin house in South Jersey, help me with repairs and build a clubhouse for Owen, and Owen would dig the underground fort in the backyard near the lilacs, and put pennies on the railroad tracks to be flattened by passing trains. Then we'd move to another neighborhood, by now with four cats in tow, to the ranch house near the swim club. Owen would be a lifeguard. Time—seven, eight years, *poof*—gone in an instant.

Life in New Jersey and at *The Philadelphia Inquirer*, where I was working as an editor, followed its course, and Jeanne and her husband got tenured at a branch of the State University of New York. We hardly spoke of the furniture, except to confirm that one of us—whichever one was currently responsible— had paid the storage bills. We already had our own houses full of furniture, including a few family things each of us had taken over time. Jeanne had the Victorian love seat and the little compote jar with the silver owl on top, the best set of family silver and the barrel chair. I had the double bed that my grandmother and grandfather had shared when they stayed in Washington with Bessie's cousin Adele. I'd put dibs on it early on, and at some point in the 1970s Mother had shipped it to me along with the bureau with the carved acanthus leaves and flowers that had held some of the tableware and daily linen in the dining room. So what were we going to do with those two storage bins full of, well, mostly antiques?

I would think of it, when I did at all, fleetingly—in stereo: There it was in the bins, but there it *really* was, gracing my grandmother's living room of a Virginia summer's evening in the days before we had air-conditioning or even saw the need for it. In an instant I'd be transported, see myself sitting on the great circular straw rug that was the living room's summer floor covering, surrounded by the furniture in the rose-patterned Dorothy Draper slipcovers. Fleetingly, like a shiver in a mirror, the furniture would come into my thoughts or my dreams, then vanish before I could even grasp it.

Then one morning I woke up in New Jersey, in that bed I'd claimed so many years earlier. On this morning, perhaps five years after Mother died, as I woke I could have sworn my grandmother was in the room, just for an instant, standing at the foot of the bed—the bed I had now hauled with me for almost twenty-five years, through good times and bad, through career shifts, a marriage and a divorce, a child growing up and a half dozen moves. Twenty-five years of anybody's life, it's a long time. This life just happened to be mine, and I had come to think of the bed as being mine too. But in fact it had been hers and my grandfather's, and there she was, just for an instant, gone almost before I saw her, like the way you sometimes think you catch an image out of the corner of your eye, but then when you turn, it isn't there. In that instant before she vanished, she was just the way I remembered her, not the young woman in the pictures, but the old lady in the last years of her life, dressed in one of those 1940s old-lady dresses with the blousy top and the buttons down the front, and the old-lady shoes.

Brief as it was, the moment precipitated the question: *Where do you want me to start?* As if she'd given me a directive, I started actively fretting about the furniture, which I knew the storage company had shifted from a temperature-controlled facility to a set of ordinary corrugated metal bins on cement flooring. The business had changed hands and changed venues, and there was really nothing to be done about that; these bins weren't even in Lexington, where we'd still occasionally visit. They were over in Staunton, thirty miles away, since that was the closest place that had bins in a fairly dry, secure location. But by now our family furniture—including the antique probably-Chippendale horsehair sofa, the alleged George Washington chair, a big assortment of good wood pieces and the less desirable veneered ones, and of course the china—had been sitting in these un-air-conditioned bins on a hillside in the Shenandoah Valley for a couple of years. It was quite the haul: Bess and Charlie's household, which was itself a distillation of their stuff and their parents' and grandparents', not to mention old Cousin Adele's, plus what was left of our own parents' more modest furnishings, and then some things from my father's family, retrieved from his mother's apartment in Washington after she died.

And, it struck me now, the box of family papers I'd packed that day was also in the bins. That probably wasn't good, given the age of its contents and the fact that somewhere in the hastily sorted documents and photographs were probably our last best clues to who we were, where we'd come from, and why we'd lugged all this furniture with us. Could I find them in two bins full, probably stacked to the ceiling? I'd deliberately picked a slightly larger box than most of the packing cartons the movers had brought. It was a large box, about two feet square, an ugly shade of gold, with some red writing on it. I hoped I was remembering that right.

So it was that I made the first trip to visit the furniture, five years after we'd consigned it to the bins. And at the storage company, who should be sent with me to open the bins but Roger. He showed me a shortcut from the company's business office on a drab industrial stretch of highway to the hillside where the bins stood. He remembered us, and oh, yes, our china, well. We joked about that day as he helped me figure out which key went to which bin. The metal door slid up, and there it all was, professionally arrayed in storage blankets, carefully packed and stacked.

All I could see was feet. But oh, those feet. Carved and clawed, dainty and ponderous, each bespeaking so eloquently the greater whole, sweeping me up in their synecdoche, so sweet, so freighted. Roger hovered, solicitous as an undertaker. Did I need anything moved? Unwrapped? No, I thanked him, I didn't need anything unwrapped. I knew it all by heart. The box of documents—the paper trail of our family's military hegira—was there, just as I'd remembered it. He helped me load it into the car. Together we reached for the sliding door. It rattled softly, gratingly, as I watched the feet disappear.

The trip emboldened me to think about the practicalities of paying a couple of hundred dollars a month—not so much, really, until you started adding it up—for furniture we weren't using, didn't need, and which was, after all, old. How long could we really expect it to last, there in the seasonal heat and cold? Could we let go of it? Were we brave enough for, well, an auction or something?

That summer living room with the straw rug would never be again. And the amalgamation of ancestral households was not being improved by sitting in a bin, deteriorating one chip and mouse nibble at a time. On my visit with Roger, even without unswaddling things, I'd seen some evidence of both.

Back from the trip to Virginia, I call my sister. *It's about the bins*, I tell her. *Do you have a better idea?* she says. We talk. Neither of us has room for it. It's dying there by degrees. We agree: Perhaps we could sell it—get some money we could use for something else. Let someone else have the use of it. It feels like setting doom in motion.

At a gathering a few days later, I mention my ambivalence to my friend George. George tells me how attached he's become to a serving dish he's found at an antiques shop: not a particularly valuable one, but he has begun to feel responsible for its well-being, to think about whom it might have belonged to and what they would have served in it.

This is precisely the problem. Things, alas, take on lives of their own. In its simplest form, Americans struggle with the dilemma every day, as the books on clutter and household management in any bookstore will attest. We're a material culture, dimly longing for simplicity. But as I begin to approach the problem with kid gloves on—the trip to the storage bins has left me in a stew of affectionate frustration—I see the

problem as a spiritual and not a cosmetic one. The walls are alive with the silent sounds of objects echoing our own lives back to us. We *are* our clutter, and.it is us.

I call an antiques dealer, who recommends an auction house. On the day that Pat—partner in an elegant auction house at the heart of neighboring Charlottesville's horse country—meets me at the bins, Owen and David are with me. Owen is about to graduate from high school, David is living in Virginia, and the odds are really against our all being together again before the auction. This is pretty much it.

I've somehow imagined that the boys would tell me if there was anything in the bins they absolutely had to have, anything we should hold back from the auction. Silly of me, I realize later. They don't *know* the furniture; to them all this stuff was just Grandma's—my mother's, as they had known it in her house—and they have not lived on it, in it, and with it the way the rest of the family before them did. They haven't memorized it, and to stand there and look at it all swaddled in the quilted movers' blankets doesn't speak to them the way it speaks to me.

Later, when we are in the middle of the auction, David will quietly mention, as the dishes go on the block, that he's always loved the Canton china. *Ouch*. The Canton china was one thing my sister and I were sure we didn't need, and there was so *much* of it. It was part of the "good" category of stuff, things we were also sure would fetch a price, make the buyers feel the trip had been worth their time. Still later, Owen will ask if we'd kept the twin beds. Well, yes, but one of them had been irremediably cracked in its journey through various bins and trucks and many hands. And we'd kept the beds only because we were sure they'd fetch nothing. Who'd want an old pair of mahogany twin beds? *Ouch*.

Again, and too late, I'll be reminded just how sticky is the task of unloading family possessions. One family member's trash is inevitably another's treasure. My friend Cheryl, when I tell her, instantly sympathizes. In her mother's basement is the lime-green sofa from the 1950s. No one dares dispose of it, because it is sacred to their growing-up time, and one or another member of the family would be heartbroken to see it go. But at the same time, no one *quite* has room for a long 1950s "modern" couch, especially a lime-green one—the height of fashion in its day—in their living room just at the present moment. *Right.*

So there we are at the bins, and Pat begins assessing. He's the Powell of the auction firm of Harlowe-Powell, a prominent Central Virginia auction house for fine arts and antiques, and he's actually Vernon, but he goes by Pat. For much of his appraisal of whether we'll be worth a full, well-publicized auction, he has only—like me—to look at the feet of the well-wrapped furniture. But where I see family in those feet, he's reading value. *Mm-hmm. Possible Chippendale. Probable Victorian. Good wood.* Stopping at a very large rectangular piece that, unlike the others, has no feet, he peels back the blanket to inspect. It's the sandalwood chest that for all those years in my grandparents' and then my parents' house held the good table linens. The "sandai" chest, we called it, deriving the name from the pungently sweet smell of the sandalwood, a precious and even sacred wood in the Orient with which storage chests were often lined to scent their contents and keep pests at bay.

With its beautiful, thinly hammered iron frieze of what I thought of as dragons on the front, it was always alluring and mysterious. But at the storage bins, Pat Powell doesn't spend much time on the iron frieze that has captivated me from early childhood. He sees something in the chest that we had never noticed, a clue that evokes the battlefield in a way we hadn't even thought of. What he seizes on, literally, are the handles. Not the handles that adorn the front of the chest's drawers, flanking the exuberant creatures. No, Pat immediately spots

The sandai chest

and pulls up two handles we have never even noticed. My grandfather may have known they were there. He probably did, because these were a telltale signature of the campaign chest, the essential carryall for a nineteenth-century ranking officer's effects, transported behind the scenes at the battlefield and delivered to his tent by enlisted men or coolies.

These handles are all but invisible. Flat, U-shaped beaten iron, they slide—when not in use—down into the sides of the chest through an iron-sleeved slot at the edge of the top surface. To the uninitiated eye, the iron slot at each end of the top surface merely looks like a bit of decoration. The handles would remain hidden until the bearers pulled them up to load the chest onto a wagon headed for the next battle.

I imagine that the chest may have come into Charlie's possession when he was part of the American campaign in China that took him to the heart of Peking's Forbidden City. Handy for maps, a good place to keep your clothing safe and dry, with the square locking cabinet section next to the lower drawers perfect for bottles of medicine and brandy. Beautiful to look at, too good to leave behind. Load it on an oxcart, carry it across the dusty miles to Canton, and on back to Manila, where it would help furnish the quarters of a young officer and his wife and make for a good story besides, the first of many.

As we stand with the auctioneer, it is, I realize, the beginning of some end, and for that I am actually grateful in a weird way. It's a relief to embrace the idea that the family's centuries-long accumulation of material goods is no longer going to be our personal responsibility, my sister's and mine. Never mind that we've presided over it during what may be the most material century in human history. We can and will let go, prying our emotional fingers off the mother lode.

But for now, on this spring day at the bins, I am hoping that David and Owen will stake their claims to a significant piece or two. David takes a small primitive wooden statue, and Owen a little circular wooden box with an inlaid lid. And do I have the presence of mind to protest, to shout, *But don't you want something* big? *What about the sandai chest?*

No, I don't. And like Mother with her stiff upper lip, we all just forge on. I don't mention the Canton, and neither does David. I don't offer Owen a set of beds—why would I, he has a perfectly good bed at home, and he doesn't tell me that these beds are his enduring memory of Grandma's house. This habit of keeping it all in—is it military, is it Victorian, is it merely American dysfunctional? Whatever it is, it is truly part of what they left us. What they left us was everything—and nothing. They left their belongings; what money they had; their good name and a nodding acquaintance with the trivia of civilization; a few stacks of chatty letters.

Their inner lives, those we can only guess at. You saved face; you had your space. If intimacy is reckoned in secrets shared at midnight, count us out. We rarely speak of what is in our hearts at the crucial moment.

Driving back to New Jersey, I reflected on the process of triage, on the fate of the Canton plates and the horsehair sofa and the George Washington chair. The problem wasn't that they were old or valuable. The problem was that they had become part of the family, standing in for those who didn't speak for themselves. They were the medium for a peculiar layered intimacy that continues, even though the people with whom we commune have been dead for decades. For centuries, in some cases. The furniture and the people, we are truly intertwined.

Chapter 4

THE SPOILS OF WAR

T HE SANDAI CHEST IS EMBLEMATIC OF MY GRANDPARENTS'
lives together, perhaps one of the first pieces they acquired after they married. Or more precisely, that *he* acquired. The
sandai, and an intricately carved dark wooden trunk we called
the Spanish mission chest, were part of the spoils of war.

They met in Manila in 1899. Charles was a soldier who'd
come to the islands with an invading American army, a volunteer in the U.S. Army Signal Corps and already hell-bent for
glory. Bess, her mother, and her two sisters were stranded
there: Harry Egbert had just been killed in battle, and the war
he'd come to fight—the Philippine Insurrection or Philippine-
American War—was still raging.

Like Bess, Charles Kilbourne Jr. was a U.S. Army "brat,"
the second son of a career officer. Charles Sr. had spent long
years post–Civil War stuck at the grade of major, moving his
family from one ramshackle Army post to another, before finally ending up prosaically back in Ohio, teaching military science at the state university just a few miles from where the
Kilbournes had settled in 1802. Life in the peacetime military is
hell on hopes for promotion.

Bess Egbert's father had fared marginally better in rank, thanks largely to his recklessness in battle—a trait he shared with the son-in-law he would never meet. By the time the U.S. Expeditionary Forces invaded the Philippines in 1898, on a quest to grab those island colonies from Spain and gain a base in the Pacific, Harry Egbert was already a colonel—actually a temporary brigadier general, since ranks tended to go up during combat.

By then, America was expanding its reach halfway around the globe, partly as a result of having declared war on Spain in the Caribbean earlier in the year, after the sinking of the American warship *Maine* in Havana harbor in February. The loss of the *Maine* had paid off handsomely for the aggrieved United States, as it turned out. Paradoxically? Or perhaps as the result of shrewd political calculation? President McKinley had seized on the ship's destruction as the perfect pretext to invade Cuba. Once past the heat of battle, which got virtually the whole of the American people rallying behind their wartime president, it became immaterial that no one could say for sure whether the explosion that sank the *Maine* actually had anything at all to do with Spain.

McKinley's orders at the outset of the war called for 125,000 fighting men, and Harry Egbert was among those who would lead ranks of raw recruits into battle. In Cuba, he'd take the Sixth Infantry up a steep slope called San Juan Hill, just below the fortress of Santiago. There he was wounded and left for dead for most of a day under a July sun. The "Fighting Colonel," they called him. He was always right out there on the firing line, when his proper place as a commanding officer was in the rear. As Colonel Egbert fell, Teddy Roosevelt swept in with his Rough Riders from nearby Kettle Hill to finish leading the charge. The day was won, along with instant fame for the young Roosevelt.

Triage was how Harry Egbert escaped death that day. By nightfall, he'd been lying out on the field, probably in a woolen uniform, for at least six hours when the orderlies came around. Their grim task: to identify the living and to assess. Haul the ones with the best chance of survival off to a field hospital.

"I think this one's alive," one of them reportedly said, prodding the prostrate form.

"I am resting quite comfortably," the delirious Egbert dreamily replied. "I do not wish to be moved." They moved him anyway, and he somehow survived a bullet through the lung, only to die less than a year later in the Philippines.

For after McKinley's successful gamble on ousting the Spanish from Cuba, the president set his sights on an even grander mission: A youthful United States, barely a century past being a colony itself, would now step out to rival the Europeans—the British in India, the French in Indochina. There was wealth and power to be had in the Orient. He sent his victorious American boys onward under Admiral Dewey to drive the Spanish from their Philippines colony, far out in the Pacific.

The Spanish fell easily to Dewey's fleet in May 1898, and their land forces capitulated in August, but the Filipino insurgents who had been stubbornly battling their Spanish overlords since 1896 proved to be the wild card in McKinley's plan. They'd initially joined the Americans, whom they saw hopefully as allies, in their quest to be rid of the Spanish. But the Filipinos soon created a second war of independence, this time against the Americans, as it became clear that their apparent liberators were in no hurry to leave. Harry Egbert, just six months past his near death in Cuba and still pale and thin, somehow wangled a command in a second Philippines-bound expeditionary force that would sail in January 1899 to subdue the rebels.

And this time, Harry's war-weary wife, who knew his penchant for battle all too well, went with him. Nelly Egbert packed up their family too—the girls by now in their twenties—and as much of their belongings as they could reasonably carry with them. The Orient, exotic and dangerous, was half a world away, but at this point in their lives, she did not intend to remain behind doing needlework on a godforsaken domestic post while Harry went off on another death-defying mission.

Was she prescient? The American transport ship on which the Egberts traveled sailed into Manila Harbor in March 1899. The women and children were kept on board, the commanding general having no intention of letting them roam around the capital city looking for lodgings while the rebels were still a threat. After nine days out in the field, the men came back to barracks in Manila for a three-day respite from battle, and the regiment's wives and children were let off the ship. Families had hardly been reunited when the troops were sent back out. Just days later, Brigadier General Egbert died in a wildly confused skirmish on a narrow plain before the rebel stronghold, Malolos, just north of Manila.

The women soldiered on. Reading what's left of the family records, one wonders if they even paused to mourn, so quickly did they get on with their lives. Nelly Egbert soon started a circulating book collection for the troops that would eventually grow to twenty-five thousand volumes and become the basis of the Philippines national library. Bessie immediately wrote to friends at home about her father's death, then went out and got a job in a school set up for Filipino children, where she resorted to drawing pictures to surmount the language barrier.

And sometime after the sad, bright April day in 1899 when the little family stood on the pier watching Harry Egbert carried aboard for his final voyage home—probably within just a few months of that day—Bess would meet the promising young officer who appeared to be almost as reckless as her father. Charles Kilbourne, however, was not destined to die in battle, and we grandchildren would come to know him well.

❈

CHARLIE, AS FRIENDS AND family called him, had volunteered for the U.S. Signal Corps at the outbreak of the Spanish-American War, and went to the Philippines as a Signal Corps lieutenant in July 1898. For an ambitious young man who had not attended West Point—which would have given him an automatic commission in the regular Army—it was a gamble, and a dangerous one. During the same month that Harry Egbert fell in battle, Charlie was out on reconnaissance, slogging through mountain passes and leech-infested swamps in the back country, where the Filipino revolutionary leader Emilio Aguinaldo had retreated from Manila.

But Lieutenant Kilbourne made the most of his gamble, and it paid off. His daring in one particular battle had made him famous in the whole American Expeditionary Force and won him notice even in Washington, D.C., where a Congressional Medal of Honor was being struck for the young Signal Corps volunteer who'd shinnied up a telegraph pole two times—some said three—under heavy insurgent fire to mend the essential

Charles Evans Kilbourne

The origin of Bessie's gown in this wedding portrait remains a mystery.

communication wires that the rebels had cut. More important from the practical Lieutenant Kilbourne's point of view, the deed had also earned him the promise of a commission in the *real* Army. Young Kilbourne came out of the Filipino bush in June 1899 just in time to go to the States to receive his Medal of Honor and the much-sought-after Army commission. It must have been soon after his return to the islands that he and Bessie met. In less than a year they'd be married.

He was darkly handsome. She was a natural redhead. Almost a strawberry blonde, really, with freckles, a winsome smile, and the scarred cheek she concealed with a casual hand, or by turning her head at a slight angle, her quizzical glance catching your eye and distracting you for a moment, just long enough to get you past that little deformity.

When and how, in the social whirl of the military now occupying the old Spanish capital, did they meet? And was it love at first sight? At twenty-six, she was no longer a girl, and with eligible young officers coming, going, and dying in what would soon be three consecutive wars, time was getting short. She had already been jilted once. When or by whom? An officer in Wyoming during the long winter when her father was fighting the Sioux and she had just turned seventeen? Or perhaps a Cincinnati dandy in the six years they'd spent at Fort Thomas, Kentucky? All we know is that the cut was deep enough not to be forgotten. The women of the family passed the story on, a cautionary tale.

Whatever she'd learned from the encounter, Bess would likely have had the advantage of romantic experience over young Lieutenant Kilbourne, who'd spent his late teens and early twenties at an all-male (of course) military school and the intervening years as a disciplinary officer on Indian reservations and as a weather scout in the Pacific Northwest, where suitable young ladies were in short supply.

Despite years of subsequent accomplishments that reflected his talent for strategy and his military savvy, Charlie had a certain social guilelessness until the day he died. So was it love at first sight for the two of them, or something more like expediency for the young woman who'd just lost her father to the Philippine Insurrection (as it was then called), and who now saw an American invasion of China looming, for heaven's sake, as news came of atrocities against Western missionaries on the Chinese mainland? Expediency, or love? Perhaps a bit of both.

What's certain is that when Charles's parents back in Ohio learned that he'd married some young woman immediately before shipping out to China to fight the Boxers—married her without so much as a formal invitation or announcement to family and friends, and so hastily that apparently she didn't even have a proper wedding dress—the Kilbournes were not pleased.

The Boxer Rebellion, as it was called, pulled Charlie's regiment out of the Philippines in June 1900 to join British, Japanese, Russian, and other international forces in a march on Peking. They went to lift the "siege of the Legations"—the foreign embassies and their dependents quartered near the Forbidden City portion of the Chinese capital. The insurgent attackers were a Chinese revolutionary movement determined to expel the European and American barbarians who'd disrupted Chinese life and custom with their missionaries and their gunboats. Westerners baffled by their hand-to-hand fighting discipline—what we would now call martial arts—

could only compare it to the sport of boxing, hence "Boxers." Bands of Boxers had attacked outlying missionary settlements of *fan kwei*—or *fan gui*, translated "foreign devils," "foreign ghosts" (perhaps a reference to their pale skin), or just plain "unwelcome foreigners"—with fury before engulfing Peking. European powers, including Russia, and the United States reacted with equal fury.

No one who knew my grandfather in later years would have thought of him as a violent man. Children and animals loved him. The most unmanageable horses were docile around him. Kids were fascinated by the way he could wiggle his ears and blow smoke rings. He'd invent an animal out of a napkin. He taught me to skip and took me to the creek to feed the ducks and throw Osage oranges into the stream. A picture of us when I'm about five, with my Dale Evans outfit and gun, shows him kneeling on the patio in his white linen suit, his hands raised high above his silver head.

And yet. And yet he fought in four wars, and in at least one had killed a man, or perhaps several, stalking a German machine gun nest in the nighttime fields of World War I, for which he earned the French Croix de Guerre. The etched glass in the right lens of his spectacles masked the fact that he'd lost that eye in a trench mortar explosion in France. In his wartime daring, I see his impulsive nature, a certain imperious impatience to just get the job done, whatever it was, with a reckless disregard for consequences. In the time we knew him, it would manifest itself in the way he drove a tenpenny nail into the plaster to hang a picture, or the night he heard my mother in the front hall and came out brandishing his pistol, taking her for an intruder.

He was the author of two sets of children's books, one featuring baby animals sweetly clad in Babar-style garments. The other set, however, drew on his experiences in war. In one of his books of boys' fiction—part of a series he wrote around the time of World War I about his adventures in China and the Philippines—he describes the wild feeling of exhilaration at the beginning of a battle. But he also recounts the tedious and sometimes sordid daily side of war, and its horrors—the crowded voyage from the Philippines; the long march inland to Peking, during which men fell sunstruck by the road; and the assault on the Forbidden City, in which he focuses on a particularly gruesome battle fought by Russian expeditionary forces: "Piled nearly to the height of the wall, and covering many square yards of the courtyard, were hundreds of corpses, mostly Chinese, though a few Russians were intermingled. It told the story of a fearful struggle on the wall above, in which the Russians had gained the mastery and had hurled their enemies into the courtyard below. . . . From the pile the blood still came in a sluggish stream, which passed under the feet of the crowded soldiers."

The American brigades arrived in time to help occupy Peking and maintain order, and to Charlie fell the job of policing the American sector. He writes home to his father in a letter postmarked San Francisco, but bearing the inscription "Soldier's letter—Chas. E. Kilbourne Jr. 2nd Lieut. 14th Infantry with U.S. Forces in China":

You have had full news of our fighting by this time. . . . We did noble work, too, and stand high with the other nations, in spite of our poor equipment and staff. About a week ago, our colonel sent for me and asked me how I should like to be Chief of Police. I told him I didn't want it but he detailed me anyhow. I received no instructions excepting a bundle of proclamations in Chinese which I was to distribute over the district and a translation of them . . . the Chinese were to resume business under our protection . . . looting was to be stopped—Chinese caught looting or bearing arms were to be shot. I asked for a company to be detailed each day . . . and made out orders to maintain the quiet . . . the place was filthy and full of dead men and animals. I have had it cleaned. But it is a mean job. I sat in judgment on two Chinese this morning, condemned and had them executed. It was the hardest thing I ever had to do. I have flogged and have had flogged about 50 of them. It is dirty work but unless I hold them hard I cannot control them. I am praying that we may soon be ordered away.

In the same letter he apologizes for not having informed his parents in advance of his marriage to my grandmother on the eve of his departure from Manila for China, months earlier. "You know long before now that Bessie and I did not wait for any wedding dress—clothes were about the last thing we thought of at the time." He then reproaches his father for some apparent criticism of their haste: "I was terribly cut up for awhile though I understood you all very well. The later letters though have fixed everything up . . . and now I am dead anxious to get home to you and bring her with me so that we'll all get used to it."

Reading between the lines, I imagine the slowness with which this family quarrel traveled back and forth by steamer across the Pacific Ocean. How socially inappropriate was the hasty wedding? A wife could make or break an officer's career. Did they fear for his future? Did they think she was pregnant?

When I unearth pictures of Charlie's parents, Charles Sr. and Ada look like a pretty dour pair. I remember then how Charlie would say that his mother always told her children that her oldest son, Lincoln, was her favorite. The issue of the wedding dress, meanwhile, remains a mystery. There are photos of Bessie in bridal garb. Were they posed after the fact? Or—heaven forbid—did she *borrow* a dress, when a proper young woman would have waited to have one made, or to have her own mother's or grandmother's gown sent from home?

Charlie concludes his letter with astonishing understatement from the blood-drenched streets of Peking: "There's nothing much to write of. I keep perfectly well, and am preparing for the winter in case we have to stay here."

⊁∥⊱

AT WORK ONE DAY in our newsroom at *The Philadelphia Inquirer*, I'm editing a story by one of our reporters, a Chinese American woman, about her family's role in China's early twentieth-century history. Her article touches on the Boxer Rebellion, and as we edit that section, I reveal a small part of my own family's imperialist past. Careful not to say too much, as I'm all too aware that my ancestors were on the wrong side of most of the wars they fought, I nonetheless feel compelled to tell her that I have a share in her past, her China, the China of her great-uncle Watchman Nee. I tell her that my grandfather was there as a young soldier.

Her eyes widen slightly and she laughs. "Ohhh," she says, knowingly. "You were one of the *bad* guys."

The bad guys. Yes, those would be the American armies of the Gilded Age. We never knew exactly why our grandparents referred to the big, ornately carved dark wooden chest with the domed lid and the iron hasps as the Spanish mission chest.

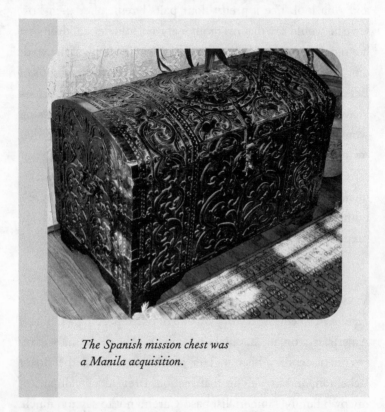

The Spanish mission chest was
a Manila acquisition.

Just the sound of it was so dramatic, conjuring up the Spanish Empire with its far-flung Pacific possessions, the Philippine Islands. Surfing the Internet, I come upon a description that sounds quite a lot like the "mission chest": "A Spanish Colonial or Philippine carved walnut chest . . . late 17th/18th century with domed top, all sides elaborately carved with scrolling and fruiting vines interspersed with exotic beasts, birds, the front with large, pierced and engraved circular iron lockplate (hasp detached), key missing . . ."

Later, I'll actually see a very similar chest in Malacanang Palace in Manila, the Philippines' seat of state. An antiques dealer tells me that Filipino artisans copied the early Spanish designs for wealthy Filipino families. I imagine both the mission chest and the sandai chest separated from their rightful owners in the chaos of war and ending up either in the American army's baggage train—in the case of the sandai chest—or, for the mission chest, in a furniture dealer's hands, to be sold to an American officer's family once things settled down.

As I work my way through the family documents, I come across still more piles of clippings about Harry Egbert—the father who had died before Bessie ever met Charlie. The one that catches my eye is a long front-page account in *The Cincinnati Enquirer* of how he died. The article contains excerpts of Bessie's letter about her father, quoted verbatim. I am struck by the placid pride with which she claims the importance of his death, heaping the garlands of heroism and decorous mourning upon her mother—his grieving widow—and on herself and her sisters in the process.

Reading it, you also feel the breathlessness of a new technology bursting to show us just how splendid and important it is. SADDENED, reads the *Cincinnati Enquirer* headline, BY THE FATEFUL WORDS, FLASHED UNDER THE OCEAN FROM MANILA . . . Imagine! News of this local Cincinnati hero's death *flashed* across an ocean and a continent for your morning reading. The same excitement and bravado infuse Charlie's accounts of battle in his books, *The Army Boy in the Philippines, The Army Boy in Pekin*. There is an assumption of rightness, of the righteousness of this invasion of the Philippines and all that lies beyond. Perhaps never again would America be so sure of itself and its destiny.

For the Americans who were repeatedly stationed abroad— my grandparents were sent to the Philippines on five separate tours of duty—life overseas conferred enormous privilege: servants, status, entrée to the world of the local aristocracy, these were automatic perquisites for officers. There was also a sense of longing, for some place that finally would be home. Yet when home was finally attained, there was a longing for what had been. My grandfather went back to the Philippines as a civilian—for what he must have known would be his farewell visit—when he was eighty-four. He found the last house they'd lived in there, devastated by the Japanese bombing of World War II and left to crumble on Corregidor. He brought back a piece of carved stone from the garden steps. It stayed on the mantel in his bedroom until he died.

And the wooden chests—the mission chest and the sandai chest—how many times did they travel back and forth across the Pacific during all those tours of duty before finally coming to rest on a continent far from their origins? The mission chest was always in his and Bessie's bedroom, where it held linens and blankets; the sandai chest had pride of place in our dining room. Long after they had both died, it was still redolent of candle wax and Bessie's ironed table linens, scents that mingled with the sandalwood's peculiar peppery sweetness.

The broken stone, I think, bespoke the hope, or perhaps the illusion, that this transient military family could, finally, belong somewhere. The wooden chests told another story: of conquest, the spoils of war.

Chapter 5

NEW JERSEY 2002:
THE ARMY TRUNK

WE SET THE AUCTION IN MOTION EARLY IN THE SPRING
of 2002, on that visit to the storage bins with Pat Powell. A
date was yet to be chosen. The furniture went to a storage bin
in Charlottesville, to be near the auction house, which occupied a towering old brick mill building, gutted to give the auction space high ceilings and lots of light. The firm's appraiser,
an energetic, businesslike woman named Sam, began the work
of assessing what this hoard might be worth.

Meanwhile, the retrieval of the family things—even
though most of them had gone to Charlottesville—had caused
some tectonic shifts back at my pleasant but modest New Jersey rancher, as I brought back still more boxes of family mis-
cellany. Our house dated from the 1960s, and its storage
capacity was perfectly adequate for perhaps two or three people with a 1990s quantity of stuff. And we had that. We had
what you'd expect: furniture and dishes, clothes and appliances, beach chairs and sleds and lacrosse sticks. Musical in-
struments. Amp and speakers for a bass guitar. A basket of
knitting stuff. A box of fabric. Computers and filing cabinets

and a fax machine. Books. Lots of books, and way too much unsorted, unprocessed paper—magazines and newspapers and clips and old book manuscripts and sample term papers for use in composition classes. Art supplies and laundry baskets and a Ping-Pong table. Garden tools and potted plants. Furniture we didn't use but for some reason hadn't gotten rid of, like the old kitchen table and my son's old bunk beds, now disassembled. Furniture left by the folks we bought the house from, in the basement and too heavy for me to move. Tons, in fact, of stuff we could probably get rid of if only we had the time—like most of our fellow Americans.

And now there were the boxes of stuff I'd brought back from the family furniture's latest move to its final set of storage bins—air-conditioned bins, now that it was almost too late to matter. The boxes were full of things the auctioneers had no interest in selling, or things the family needed to look at first. So despite the fact that our house was already full to the gills, I had to find storage space for several more cartons of pictures, books, knickknacks, and yes, more papers.

Owen would graduate in a few months and leave for college, and I was undoubtedly, in the best family tradition, in complete denial about how much I would miss him. People kept asking me if I was okay and I kept blithely telling them that yes, I was fine. So the matter of the auction was a great distraction. But it was also true that what with Owen's graduation, and the need to get him outfitted for college, all while working a full-time job, there wasn't a lot of time to prepare for the auction, and I was starting to feel as if it were bearing down on us full tilt. There was still all this sorting to be done, trying to figure out as many pieces of the family jigsaw puzzle as possible before the clues themselves were tossed aside—or sold.

And so one rainy spring Sunday afternoon, I opened up the new batch of stuff and pulled out all the documents, pictures, and other fragile papers from the box I'd retrieved from the original bins that day with Roger. I'd stuck them in some plastic storage tubs under the hall counter without ever really looking at them. My plan: not really to look at them yet, but to condense, to pack them all together more efficiently, and somehow find space for them until I had time—just a little time, someday really soon, for sure—to sift.

As I assembled the plastic tubs and the newly arrived boxes, I knew I was giving up the rest of the day, and I'd be lucky if I got through it that quickly. A cursory assessment revealed letters; documents rolled up in tubes that, when I pulled them out, I saw were family trees written out in two sets of handwriting, my mother's near the bottom and someone else's in the earlier sections; typed biographies of family members including Charlie and Harry Clay Egbert; and handwritten pages that included what appeared to be a funeral oration delivered in Manila in 1913 in memory of Nelly Egbert.

There were also at least two boxes that contained mostly family photographs but also several flags or pennants I'd never seen before. Given the family history, they were almost certainly military. More to the point, since I had never seen them or the papers and pictures before, they were definitely older than I was and getting more fragile by the minute.

Our 1960s closets were crammed. The attic was the kind with no floorboards, just joists and plaster. No good putting papers and pictures in the basement, where they'd mildew. A trunk that we were using as a coffee table in the family room offered a solution. I knew I'd thrown some gowns from the 1970s into it last time we'd moved, which was about three years after Mother died. They could go to the basement, liberating a good ten or twelve cubic feet of storage space.

So—the trunk. Kneeling, I pry open the lid. The trunk is olive drab, its seams reinforced with metal strapping and rivets, my father's name and rank—he was a captain the day the Quartermaster staff block-lettered his particulars on it—in bold, laconic black between two red stripes. It traveled with us, my sister and me, to camps and colleges, and I'd only recently torn the last tattered remains of a Railway Express tag from one of its latches.

I lift out the gowns, four of them, all spun from the same faux-satin polyester of the disco era. Some padding from a coat hanger has decayed all over one of them, but my dismay is focused not on those crumbs of ruin, but on what lies beneath. From the ubiquitous gray flannel bags and the scent of sandalwood that permeates them, I know that I have stumbled on a cache of family silver. Damn. I remember now, I brought it back when we closed Mother's house and I had to put it somewhere. We were almost as short of space then as we are now. So into the trunk it had gone, where it was quickly and thoroughly forgotten.

Almost against my will, I reach in. It is opening Pandora's box to go there, but what am I to do? My plan for the afternoon revolves around wresting a little order from the chaos, and the meager space this trunk affords is my current best hope.

I lift out a bag. Its contents are lumpy, knobby, and light. I am relieved. It's only the napkin rings; they're small, we can find a place for them. I pull out the silver napkin ring with the broken butterfly poised on top. Then the square one my mother used, that was her mother's before her. Then two from West Point, my father's and his father's.

As I turn my father's USMA napkin ring over in my hands, I suddenly remember the story of the night my father threw

The West Point napkin ring

the ring—a good couple of ounces of sterling silver—at my mother's head. In my mother's version, they were sitting at opposite ends of the dinner table in their apartment in the Kalorama section of northwest Washington. It was sometime in the early forties, and the war was on. My father was working long hours in the Pentagon's logistics section, as that department, driven by Eisenhower, scrambled to overcome a lack of trained soldiers and matériel and ready the armed forces for a probable assault on the European continent.

Dinner hour was doubtless even later than usual on this particular night, and they had almost certainly had drinks before it. No one afterward remembered just what the subject was, but at some point my father seems to have completely lost his temper and flung the napkin ring down the table. It whistled past my mother's ear and—as she told me years later—went through the glass of the front door, reducing it to shards. "The next day," she related matter-of-factly, "your father of course went to work." They had only one car, and with gas rationed, she was hardly going to ask the neighbors to drive her to the hardware store to replace a pane that her husband had—ahem—broken with his napkin ring. So she took the measurements, caught a bus, had the glass cut, and carried the new pane back on the bus. "And of *course* it was the wrong size, and I had to go back."

When I mentioned it to my sister, several years after Mother's death, her eyes lit up. She'd been perhaps eight at the time, and remembered that evening well. "Oh, and the two of them went right out after dinner to find the thing and bring it back in so the neighbors wouldn't go out in the morning and find Max Tracy's West Point napkin ring lying out on the sidewalk. But it was wartime, of course, so the city was on air-raid alert, blacked out, pitch dark. So they get a flashlight, and they're out there in the dark, foraging around in the gutter and cursing quietly, trying not to wake the neighbors up." We fell silent for a moment, as I tried to envision my father in a rage I never knew, while she remembered a younger and more volatile pair of parents. Stubborn and proud, each in their own way spoiled, each an only child whose temper had been curbed but not broken by their Victorian parents—the irresistible force, as my mother would say, having met the immovable object.

I pause now, feeling just a bit guilty about all these sterling silver rings that were once such an everyday fixture now lying unused and unappreciated. But I rally. The next bag is an assortment of dressing table odds and ends: a hairbrush, a clothes brush, a buttonhook, a nail tool of some kind. Most bear the initial Y. That's the Young family, probably great-grandmother Nelly, she of the dramatic move to the Philippines and the library there.

I was given this dressing table set as a little girl. It must have come from Cousin Adele's house, in the first big family furniture triage. Cousin Adele had no children, and my mother's family were her closest kin. Mommy and Bessie, our Granny, would have brought them down from Washington after Adele died. I remember as I look at them that I was only four when they were given to me and that all the other women of the family—my sister, my mother, her mother—already had silver dresser sets of their own. Though I earnestly tried to be proud of having a set of my own, in truth the silver rather intimidated me, with its dull polish and its heavy Art Nouveau–looking swirls, the head of a woman entwined in flowered vines.

Women's things—they make me think now only of the middle-class set of attitudes and ideas that they imply. Of violet water, lace, and mirrors. Bureau scarves and darning eggs. Propriety, and grace, I suppose, under pressure. I set the pieces aside.

The biggest bag is a jumble of odd table silver, and it is somewhat alarming, as it serves to remind me that several other large remnants of sets are floating around somewhere down at home, in the attic of the house we've rented out.

On one of the ubiquitous gray flannel wrappers is a note in my mother's handwriting: "Six pearl-handled lunch knives."

The fork monogrammed JWW:
What was it for, anyway?

On inspection, I see that the knives do have handles that might be mother-of-pearl, lightly carved with a vaguely Oriental look. No provenance, and the blades are thin and dull, with predictably rounded ends.

In another flannel wrapper is an assortment of baby utensils, demitasse spoons, and a strange two-pronged fork marked JWW—for Jeanne West Wood, our paternal grandmother Tracy's maiden name. I stop and ponder the etiquette of initials. Which was preferable, for the engraving on a woman's silverware to reflect her maiden name or her married identity? Maiden name for sure, I think, as I recall the infamous silverware story.

When my mother and father became engaged, Big Jeanne—as we called Daddy's mother—preempted the whole matter of tableware by ordering a complete set in the Stieff Kirk "King" pattern, which she not only picked out for them (the *impertinence!*) but also had engraved, not with my mother's initials but with the *couple's* initials—E for Elizabeth, my mother's given name, M for my father, Max, and T for what was soon to be their common last name. Well, if you think *that* didn't send a message about who was in charge. Not the bride, clearly, to whom in that day the choice of household accoutrements was generally ceded. It was an affront my mother considered somewhere between tacky and downright malicious, and she never forgot it.

I'd heard from my sister the story of Mother's umbrage at her mother-in-law's high-handedness. And sure enough, years later when I finally unpacked the family attic, I found confirmation in the form of several individual pieces Mother had obviously received before her wedding, with her *own* initials on them, and one of Mother's little handwritten editorial postscripts attached—for us to find? Perhaps; "21 silver teaspoons," it reads, "7 of them given to me by my godmother, with the initials EGK, bless her heart."

My parents proceeded to use the offending silverware. Without further ado? I don't know about that; I was hardly a year old on the night the napkin ring took flight. By the time I was old enough to remember them, their personal lives had

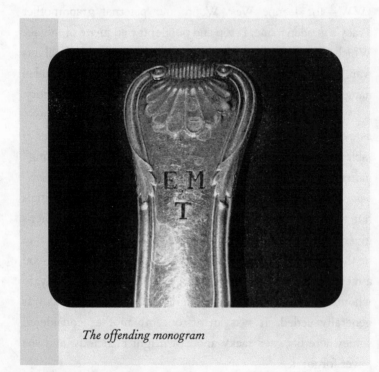

The offending monogram

settled into an almost middle-aged quiet and the EMT tableware was in daily use. But everyone agreed they fought like caged tigers in the beginning, and the silver may well have been one item on the agenda.

As the trunk sits open, the smell of sandalwood fills the room. In my parents' house, the silver had been stored at home in several chests made of the fragrant wood, and the tissue and flannel it's wrapped in are suffused with the scent. The dining room at home always had the subtle, sweet, faintly peppery undercurrent of sandalwood too—not, as I'd once vaguely supposed, a property of the napkins, mats, and tablecloths, but of the sandai chest itself. The same faint aroma hung in the living room of our neighbor across the street, an Army widow. It is the smell of my childhood.

The next batch of flannel wrappers yields two pieces of my sister Jeanne's baby silver, engraved with her name. Unless of course it's my grandmother Jeanne's, for whom my sister is named. Multiply a baby cup and spoon by all the generations that might have had such silver, and divide by the number of people with the same name, and you get an idea of how hopeless it could be to ever sort out what came from whom, or when and where.

And all these beautiful pieces lie idle and silent, not likely in our lifetimes to grace a social event. I personally don't even know what that two-pronged fork is for (a carving implement?), and it is all I can do at the pace of life we are living to haul out my parents' second set of silver—the silver plate that some company of soldiers serving under Daddy gave them as a parting gift—for the occasional Christmas dinner.

So what? Quit whining and sell it. Donate it to a cause. Would anyone want Jeanne West Wood's solitary fork from what I guess would be the turn of the century? (Much later, I'll be told it was a pickle fork.) And what of the single salt spoon and the smattering of demitasse silver? There's no demitasse in *our* lives. We drink our coffee by the mugful as we sprawl in the living room after those rare holiday dinners when the members of our small family have managed to assemble in one place. Again, as I sit with the silver refugees bundled in their gray flannel, I feel my resistance to that tug of propriety. Not for the women of my generation the silver tea service. And yet . . . how can we part with even one piece of silver—or, for that matter, china or damask or wood—until we know whose it was and why they thought it was important to keep it and pass it on?

⋇⋇

LET'S SAY YOU ARE in my mother's house anytime in the two decades after my father's death. By now the house is entirely Mother's. It's well into the second half of the twentieth century, and all of the grandparents are long gone; my sister and I have finished college and departed.

You enter the living room through an arch off the front hall, and you're face-to-face with the white Chippendale sofa, an imposing piece of furniture, and the red chair. The Egbert rocker has its back to you. The early Victorian love seat has gone off to Scotland with my sister. Its place has been taken by the rosewood love seat and lady's parlor chair, daintier and more elegant than the rest.

The rosewood pieces are latecomers, culled from grandmother Jeanne's apartment in Washington after her death sometime in the early 1960s. Mother and Daddy went up to clear out her rooms in the handsome Dresden Apartments building with its parquet floors and tall windows overlooking Connecticut Avenue. Like Charlie and Bess Kilbourne—Mother's parents—Daddy's father and mother, Joe and Jeanne Tracy, were career military. The Washington apartment had been their home in retirement. It would be the third entire household of family furniture my parents had inherited in the space of just a little more than fifteen years, and my mother was getting ruthless. Besides, she'd never quite forgiven her mother-in-law regarding the wedding silver, and now she was looking at the elegant living room and its impeccable Gilded Age accoutrements with a critical, perhaps even a hostile, eye.

I can just see them in that triage. He: *Well, we'll want to keep the sofa* . . . She, immediately vowing that the imperious Second Empire settee, the focus of Jeanne's parlor, will never grace *her* living room: *Well, I don't know where we'd put it* . . . In the end it will be banished to a neighbor's front hallway until I leave for college. Then it is relegated to my bedroom upstairs, along with Big Jeanne's writing desk, rocking chair, and very good Federal armchair. Her mahogany highboy returned with them too, to lodge uneasily in the outer corner of our dining room, the corner nearest the front door, as if ready to decamp at the first word. Mother stored some of the family's inexhaustible supply of table linens in it. Another bureau, a Sheraton with beautifully carved spirals on its front, came with them too. *God,* I'll think of my mother years later, *she must really have hated having a mother-in-law who had better furniture than she did.*

The furniture was the family's constant companion. To us, it spoke most immediately of that pivotal era of American history, the decades of our grandparents' youth and maturity, which saw America wage empire-building wars on three continents with the help of people like our own nomadic military family.

Of my four grandparents, three were themselves children of the military. And for these military families, home really was contained in the furniture. You'd arrive at a post, unpack it all, buy a few pieces on the cheap from departing officers' families—or, in places like Manila, from the local marketplaces—and set up camp in whatever quarters you'd been assigned. One retired officer from the post–World War II period has told me that "three moves was the equivalent of a fire" in terms of how much continuity a family could hope to manage during so many relocations. What with a family's packing and unpacking them at the rate of once every year, or two or three, papers and pictures and even cherished objects fell by the wayside. Memory would reside in whatever you managed to hang on to, and you'd try to hold on to it long enough to pass it on.

In this sense, military families carry the essence of our history as a nation of nomads, and what is left of the households that accompanied them on their travels bears witness to their lives—occasionally, slyly, letting drop a new tidbit, a clue, a previously undisclosed piece of the puzzle. The items in those bins in Virginia represented our last best chance of getting to know who they were, these ancestors both immediate and remote.

But in earlier times, the furniture had other stories to tell, other roles to play. As the Gilded Age unfolded, the Tracys, Kilbournes, Woods, Wests, and Egberts—the strands that composed this particular family in the making—found themselves positioned to use their family history for social advancement. The furniture, besides providing the essential façade and backdrop for social engagements, was perhaps their best ally. Nothing answered the age's mad acquisitive lust for old and exotic furnishings so well as already having them.

In this fledgling capitalist empire, as in the earlier British Empire, the best hope for bright young men of a certain class and less than enormous wealth was the military. For the military officer at home or abroad, the Gilded Age represented a signal opportunity to mix with the rich and famous on Uncle Sam's dime. There was a catch, though: Keeping up with the

Vanderbilts on an officer's pay was expected if you meant to succeed. You'd have to reciprocate invitations issued, and you'd court advancement by initiating the occasional invitation as well.

The portrait of Admiral Wood was a good conversation piece.

The bar was high. The unprecedented wealth of the era financed a luxurious lifestyle that rivaled, and liked to evoke, other over-the-top epochs such as the court of the Sun King or imperial Rome. Never notably wealthy, the tribe of military families that had produced three of my four grandparents did have a few cards to play. They'd been in the United States since before there was one—a legacy they'd perhaps done nothing to deserve, but which nevertheless impressed later, if wealthier, arrivals—and they had the stories to prove it and the manners to pull it off without appearing to actually brag. Those stories resided in part in the furniture, in family living rooms where the Empire settee and the Chippendale sofa awaited guests, and where the objects that adorned the table or hung from the walls were certain to impress.

On the Tracy side, there was the portrait of William Maxwell Wood. Big Jeanne's grandfather, he was also the Navy's first surgeon general, and there was also a pair of elegant brass ship's lamps with their etched glass shades, which would be good for a story about Admiral Wood's exploits at sea. Jeanne augmented the family artifacts with skill and style, for she had an eye for furnishings as well as clothing and didn't hesitate to tax her husband's modest military income with a fashionable love seat or some good Chinese rugs.

The furniture from Bess Kilbourne's family was as good as a dowry. The Chippendale sofa—its age confirmed under Mother's watch by a furniture expert from the Virginia state museum—likely came from a Maryland ancestor who'd served as a doctor in the Revolutionary War, and there were the so-called George Washington chair and grandpapa Daniel Egbert's ship's decanters, for he too was a naval surgeon; and of course the Egbert rocker, which would recall the family's service in the Philippines, Bess's father and his valiant final battle, and how she'd met and married Charles there, such a romantic courtship.

The age's *nouveaux riches* have come down to us as a somewhat tragicomic cast of characters, the Babbitts and their betters, largely because of their desperate earnestness to look good—in fact, to look better, richer, gayer, smarter, and more opulent than anyone else including the blue-blooded families who'd preceded them as the nation's aristocracy. In that context, people with ancestors and interesting possessions were a form of collectible in themselves. Stocking one's dinner parties with guests whose families had been here for a while was *de rigueur,* and if they happened to be young and attractive, eager and impecunious, and in uniform, so much the better.

So while young officers might be preoccupied with military advancement, with all the propriety, politicking, and personal or familial connections it demanded, the women were at work behind the scenes. Without wealth, their currency was blood: those forebears dating from the colonial era who'd fought in every generation and had left the portraits and military gewgaws to prove it.

The game of social advancement was one that Bess and Jeanne, both daughters of officers, knew well. They were in fact ideal officers' wives—healthy, attractive, intelligent but discreet, and with the training born of a lifetime in the military. Jeanne was actually quite a beauty, with dark gold hair, blue eyes, and aquiline features, which didn't hurt; Bess was less stunning, but—a keen student of people—more than made up for it with her poise and charm.

Both women married well, though not the men of their hearts' desires. Both ended up spending years in the tropics— the Philippines, Panama, and wherever else the newly minted American empire sent its armies. Elizabeth Egbert "Bess" Kilbourne and Jeanne West Wood Tracy would certainly have met as career officers' wives as early as 1920, when their husbands—both of them returning from the battlefields of World War I France—spent a year at the prestigious Army War College in Washington. The War College was part of how officers were groomed for advancement, especially in peacetime when they couldn't earn rank in battle; it was also a way of keeping good men in peacetime by offering them this special assignment.

It must have been a heady experience for the two women to arrive in the nation's capital at the end of a war and the beginning of the so very urban Jazz Age—instead of being packed off to, say, Fort Leavenworth, Kansas, where their husbands might just as well have found themselves, instead of Washington, as the Army settled into peacetime mode. But it is very likely the two women met earlier, in another glittering capital at the end of another successfully concluded war. Joe and Jeanne Tracy were posted to the Philippines shortly after Charles and Bess Kilbourne were married there in 1900. As the wives of young American officers in the capital city of Manila, they would both have responded to the invitation from "Mrs. Roosevelt" that I found in a box of my grandmother Jeanne's letters, and to the black-edged summons to a Manila memorial service after President McKinley's assassination. And there would have been many other occasions when their paths could have crossed, in Manila as well as in Washington, for they belonged to a social set that was part of the same privileged class.

Tracking their lives in the society columns of the time, you can see ample evidence of that class membership: Jeanne Tracy featured in the society pages of *The Washington Post*, while the Army's in-house newspaper reports the Kilbournes being fêted as they departed Fort Monroe for another post. Ranking Army officers and their wives were routinely invited to diplomatic and society affairs when abroad. Stateside, another scrap from Big Jeanne's trove of souvenirs reveals, they stayed at the Waldorf-Astoria. What might they have thought of each other, these two socially ambitious women, both so keen to exercise their personal charm, their household skills, their social standing, to further their husbands' careers?

On one visit to the auction house, I unexpectedly encounter a glimpse of them during their days as young Army wives when the appraiser, Sam, shows me a trove of clothing she's found among the stuff she's examining. The dresses catch my eye. They're thin, made of *jusi* (pronounced "husi"), the finely woven banana or pineapple fiber fabric of the Philippines, and floor length, with the long sleeves that a respectable woman would wear in public regardless of the weather. There are parasols too, and gloves, and a child's playsuit.

I imagine the two young Army society matrons meeting up with each other, perhaps on the fashionable Luneta promenade overlooking Manila Bay. I see Jeanne, the city sophisticate, in the black dress, with a parasol. Bess is in a less formal but still tasteful dark green and blue plaid with a thin gold thread running through it. She knows it shows off her fair complexion and that she's made the right choice; this blue and green *jusi* is something rare, unique to the place itself and perfect for her coloring. But she can't help being chagrined at her social rival's urban ease. That Jeanne—always so up to the minute, always so fashionably correct. It's hard to measure up.

At this moment, neither of them knows that they'll someday be related—by marriage. Jeanne's son, Max, won't be

*Bess Kilbourne
and
Jeanne Tracy,
circa 1900*

born for two years yet, Bess's daughter—christened Elizabeth after her mother but called Betty—for eight. At this moment, the two women are hardly more than girls themselves.

⚜

ONE WEEKEND MORNING in New Jersey, my sister, Jeanne, arrives for a visit. It's May, and I'm recently back from that meeting with Sam. The auction is on our minds as we get out the place mats and tableware for lunch. *Ah, the lunch napkins,* she says wistfully. Yes, they are the lunch napkins, the pale blue-and-white ones with their faint geometric designs. Not the sleek white dinner linen, monogrammed and embroidered; these cotton Filipino napkins were for less formal meals. One of them is in shreds, but I keep using it. We've started using the napkin rings too, my son Owen and I. I've justified both the napkins and their rings as a small gesture for the environment, at least. They bind us also, in deed and word, to long-ago lunches at Bessie and Charlie's house, homemade vegetable soup and crisp corn cakes with brown-sugar syrup. In them, my grandmother and grandfather still live, breathe, and face each other serenely from opposite ends of the dining room table ("Charles!"—reprovingly, at breakfast, as he unabashedly dunks his toast into his bowl of caramel-colored coffee, a habit he picked up in France in 1918 and she deplores).

After lunch, Jeanne and I are sitting out on my back deck. It's the season of her birthday, when it's our tradition for her to visit from upstate New York. Spring can be lovely in the Philadelphia area, in this old Quaker town that has become one of the city's South Jersey suburbs. Dogwood and redbud and star magnolias are in bloom here, while her part of New York is still locked in winter.

We're talking about the furniture now, over coffee, and why we have hung on to so much of it even though we clearly didn't have room—or even much use—for a lot of it. I tell my sister of my anxiety, as the auction approaches, for the things we've inherited. Not anxiety *about* them, I say; anxiety *for* them, like the kind of worry you'd have for your children as you sent them off from home—another preoccupation of mine at this time, of course, as Owen prepares to leave for college.

Yes, she says, because that's what it is. Anxiety *for* them because they are things that, to us, have a life. It's the only contact we have now with so much of the family, with members we've loved and lost, and those we never knew at all but who seem part of the very tissue of our lives. Our only way of touching them, the same way you'd go sit beside a gravestone. We want the things to have a good home, or a decent burial, and until they do, we feel responsible.

As it happens, we grew up in a town in the Southern mountains at a time when, as Jeanne says, the names on the street signs, the gravestones, and the mailboxes were all the same—but they weren't ours. The deep sense of continuity that existed there didn't pertain to us; we have no idea where most of our family is buried, including kin as close as aunts and uncles. Those we do know of are mostly buried too far away to be visited conveniently—Mother and Daddy at West Point, the grandparents in the maze of Arlington National Cemetery, where you need a map to get around. Great-grandparents? At least a couple in Ohio, we're not sure where, someplace north of Columbus. Aunts, uncles, cousins are scattered from the Philippines to California, from Arizona to the Pacific Northwest. One was buried at sea, another we think perhaps in the Carolinas.

And in that we are not unique. We're Americans, our lives transient and easily uprooted. Yet the ideal that we Americans cherish is some cozy picture-book town—like the Lexington of our childhoods, or some idealized New England village— where everyone knows his neighbors, and where the names on the street signs and in the cemetery are indeed your own. I think that's what makes Thomas Kinkade's paintings so popular. Seems like everyone craves that small-town fantasy, and Kinkade provides it, just as surely as Currier and Ives did in their day.

The reality is that most of us have little enough idea of where our great-grandparents are buried and even less chance of ever seeing the place we originally "came from." This is about grief and loss, says Jeanne. As a people, we grieve because we don't get to close the circle. We don't know how so many of our families' stories ended. We move around so much, sometimes we don't even know what happened to our childhood friends, to the houses we lived in, to the people we worked with just ten years ago. As a country, she says, we don't realize that our anxiety and our greed are part of an effort to lay the ghosts to rest.

She tells me a story I've never heard before. It's about her own first encounter with the sense of rootlessness. It was the year when Mother and Granny Bessie were bound for Cousin Adele's house in Washington after Adele died, for the first of the family furniture triages. By then we were settled in Lexington. Jeanne would have been about ten, and in those days she longed for our occasional trips up to Washington, where the

Tracy grandparents, who doted on her, lived. She'd spent most of her first seven years living right around the corner from their Connecticut Avenue apartment. The Kilbourne grandparents in Lexington had been a bit of a letdown. They were preoccupied with making the necessary adjustments to their lives in the wake of Charlie's recent retirement from his position as superintendent of VMI. And in any case, our grandmother Bess was not one to fuss over children.

Jeanne relates how she rejoiced at the prospective trip, only to be told rather curtly that she wouldn't be going along this time. "But I want to go *home!*" wailed Jeanne. Mother that day was probably preoccupied with the impending trip and a little irritated at the work it would entail; but she was also not one to encourage emotional outbursts of any kind. She turned on Jeanne sharply. "We—*have*—no—home," she snapped.

Jeanne remarks that these days people go out and buy old photographs, other people's photographs, because they want to have old photos sitting on their tables. *I don't like photographs,* she says. They're about the past. They represent loss, every single one of them. You don't take pictures of the bad times. You take pictures of the good times, and then you're sorry you did, because the past is past, and you can't go back and make things turn out the way you wanted. The whole country is living with unclosed loops, with unfinished stories. For us, between the family discipline of the stiff upper lip and decades of transiency, the unclosed loops are many.

We ponder: The napkins and napkin rings have set us on this particular train of thought. Like photographs, like the furniture, they are stand-ins, and vehicles. Wouldn't I be happy, I say, to give up the antique bed if I could talk with Charlie again for a day? Wouldn't we be happy, says my sister, if we could even get to the gravestones? To be able to say, so this is how they lived. This is where they died.

⚜

AS FOR THE SILVERWARE that had started me thinking about the Gilded Age—and all that it brought us, for better or worse—I lugged the bags of silver to my bedroom at the end of that long afternoon and dumped them on the closet floor. The rest of the house somehow didn't feel private enough for all the stories issuing from those soft blue and gray wrappers.

I hadn't accomplished much. Owen came out from instant messaging or something as I was putting it all back in its flannel bags and crumpled tissue-paper wrappings. He picked up the clothes brush and examined it with some curiosity. "Is it silver?" he asked. Yes, I told him, and of our family. "Wow," he said, and picked up the buttonhook. I described women's high-button shoes.

He was momentarily incredulous at the thought, then remembered why he was looking for me. He needed double-A batteries. Would I pick some up when I went to the grocery store?

I said I would. It took a few minutes, but I did return, reluctantly, from the Jazz Age, from nineteenth-century Manila, from the Washington of World War II and the heavy napkin ring through the glass door pane. I took myself off to the supermarket, where none of my fellow shoppers would have the slightest idea where this middle-aged, middle-class, jeans-clad woman had spent all of a rainy Sunday afternoon.

Chapter 6

THE THREAD OF MEMORY:
ON THE TRAIL OF
THE WASHINGTON CHAIR

THE AUCTION HOUSE STAFF SAID OUR SALE MIGHT BE A big one, and they might combine our things with one or two other lots that would complement them. By late summer we'd decided the auction would be in November or perhaps January, avoiding the winter holidays when all but a hardy few are too preoccupied to think of spending an entire day bidding on something they might not get to buy. The months between would give Harlowe-Powell the time they'd need to produce the catalog and other auction literature, like the beautiful glossy brochures they'd shown us.

Since I lived closer to Virginia, I was the contact person, doing whatever I could to help the auctioneers. On a trip to Lexington to visit friends, I stopped in Charlottesville to check with Sam, the appraiser, about some details for the brochure. I found her engrossed in the contents of a gunmetal-gray packing crate stenciled with my grandfather's initials, CEK. She was sifting through a whole pile of faded papers, and as I looked more closely, parchment. "You need to get these restored immediately," she said, with an appraiser's reckless disregard for the typical client's finances.

I thought I'd taken all the family papers out of the bins by now. These documents Sam was holding were news to me.

We gingerly unfurled one of the parchment pieces. Despite what looked like a bad spill on the top portion, and the eighteenth-century script with its unfamiliar slant and extra flourishes, I could make out the word "Indenture," plus the names of two members of the William Penn family—those founders of Philadelphia and indeed of Pennsylvania—and a name I hazily recognized as someone from our family: Saltar.

It was a Thomas Saltar. Back in New Jersey, I'd taken a cursory look at the trove of documents I'd brought from the storage bins, and I vaguely remembered seeing a name like that somewhere in the pile. But I couldn't remember which document exactly; one of the family trees? It wasn't one of the more recent names, a Kilbourne or Egbert or Young or even a Dennis, I'd know those. Maybe someone's wife? But that wouldn't be Thomas Saltar.

Even more puzzling, and interesting to us both, was the word "Indenture." As I stood over the old wooden crate with the eighteenth-century sheepskin in my hands, I could see wheels turning in Sam's head: What a great backstory if all these antiques turned out to have belonged to a family that started out as somebody's scullery maids and stable hands.

I knew that the state of Virginia in colonial days had indentured servants, but somehow I hadn't thought of the Quakers that way. But then everybody in those days had servants. Maybe our ancestors *were* part of the "downstairs" contingent? People got to America any way they could. I was baffled. Baffled and—simultaneously cognizant of all the unsorted papers already stashed back at home in New Jersey—more than a little overwhelmed by all this *new* old stuff. Trying to decipher anything beyond the word "Indenture," which was in larger letters, and the names, was just too much to deal with that afternoon. So I took the papers and parchment from Sam, dutifully thanking her for the mandate about preservation, which I knew I wouldn't be honoring anytime soon. In a sort of daze I climbed into the car for the trip back to Philadelphia.

The prospective sale of the furniture was subliminally but unspeakably stressful. The wooden crates Sam was unpacking had sat unnoticed in our basement for years. It's a miracle they didn't get carted to the sidewalk and dumped when we moved stuff out of the house. It never occurred to us that they weren't empty. Probably the only reason we kept them was a combination of sheer overwhelm and my grandfather's initials. Just taking the line of least resistance: They were Charlie's, better keep them.

As I traveled north from Charlottesville, the car began to fill with the dry, sweet, faintly musty smell of decaying paper. Family trees, deeds, wills, clippings, and pictures of nameless unlabeled ancestors filled the boxes on the floor and seat next to me.

Now as I drove, the HOV lanes to Washington announced their availability to vehicles bearing two or more occupants. I laughed quietly, thinking how my unprepossessing station wagon outstripped them all, laden with the ghosts of dozens hovering in the air around me. I was inhaling my ancestors, one dusty molecule at a time.

☒∥☒

BACK IN NEW JERSEY, I puzzle over these indentures. Since the auction house has mentioned again that any help we can provide in establishing the provenance of the furniture will of course increase its worth, I'm in the process of following all the leads I can think of in the time we have left before they print the catalog and advertise the event. Much of the furniture is clearly Victorian, and it of course will bring only whatever people are willing to pay for heavy carved pieces of good wood. If we can prove that any of the other pieces are older—or, even better, older with some historical importance—they'll fetch more. There's the Empire settee, for instance. It might be old enough to have belonged to William Maxwell Wood, the Navy surgeon general. And those black chairs with the woven bottoms and the gold painted design on the backrest are plain enough to be early nineteenth century, but we're really not sure whom they belonged to. And we're racing against the clock. I'll do what I can.

One piece I've particularly set my sights on is the George Washington chair, since it came with at least the name attached—and with the name, the claim, or at least the idea, that the chair had actually belonged to the great man—though we didn't really know when or how it had ended up in our possession.

Besides its family moniker, the GW chair is also high on the list of pieces to try to document for material reasons: Sam has taken a paint scraping from the underbelly of the chair's frame, and she says that that and its shape could qualify it as a late eighteenth-century *fauteuil*—which would increase its value even if it had no connection to Washington. But its likely age does suggest a possibly provable connection: The Washingtons lived in Philadelphia when he was president and that city was the nation's capital. I seemed to remember that Mother had mentioned at one point some branch of the family being from around Philadelphia too, and now a name on one of these indentures has confirmed that.

So who was it, exactly, who came from Philadelphia, and when? I can't dredge up a family story that's of any help. I think, on reflection, that the dinner table was about the only place where the family were all assembled at the same time— Mother, Daddy, Charlie, and us children—and where family stories came into the conversation. The rest of the time— when they weren't at work or lugging Jeanne or me to school, church, choir practice, or whatever—it was pretty much understood that the grown-ups would appreciate having some time to themselves, and we were expected to do the same. Go do some homework or read a book. Study for a spelling bee. Paint a picture.

And at the dinner table, there was so much recent family history, peppered with so many moves from one post to another, with so many war stories—especially Charlie's—that we never even got back as far in the family lore as the Civil War, much less to a bunch of parchment that someone had thrown into a wooden crate in the basement, or to the question of who might have acquired the George Washington chair.

And so, the indentures. If this pile of parchment can help solve the riddle of the chair's provenance, now's the time to start trying to decipher it. The handwritten eighteenth-century script is elegant but cramped, and, when I next tackle it, still hard to read. But as I keep at it, I realize that it's a contract for land, not for servants. I look up "indenture" in Merriam-Webster, and its first meaning is just that: a contract. So this indenture of Saltar's is actually a deed, to property in what in the late 1990s became the trendy Northern Liberties section of Philadelphia. As I pick through it, I see that Thomas Saltar was deeded his property in the Liberties by two Penns who, it appears from a quick look on the Internet, were likely a nephew and a grandson of the great William Penn himself, serving as the proprietors and therefore the dispensers of land deeds for the colony of Pennsylvania. The date of the deed is 1765.

I've worked at the *Inquirer* in Philadelphia now for almost twenty years, and I know from a project I'd done for the paper in 1987, for the bicentennial of the Constitution, that the Liberties—now a fashionable neighborhood of galleries and restaurants—actually stood in those days outside, just to the north, of the city proper. The Liberties were the place you went to get away from downtown, where Quaker proprieties held sway. They were, in short, the "anything goes" district of the 1700s. By Quaker standards, of course, that could simply have meant where the taverns were located, since the worthy Friends had a testament (the Quakers' name for their affirmations of their beliefs) against alcohol in any form. So, I think, what does it say about this ancestor that he was a Northern Liberties landowner?

I'm intrigued. In my imagination, Thomas Saltar transmogrifies from indentured laborer to bawdy-house owner, or at the very least saloon keeper. He and his deed are right now the most promising connection I've found between George

Washington, who spent his second term as president in Philadelphia, and our family's chair. The date, 1765, at least puts Saltar in the city in the decade leading up to the American Revolution. This in itself may be a slender thread, but it's enough to keep me going.

The deeds are old and stiff. As I open them and other documents, the dust from the parchment and papers coats my eyeballs and fills my nose and mouth with a fine film. But I feel obliged to get through them all before I shove the boxes under a counter in our hall, so at least I'll know whether there are any leads worth following.

Next I come across a faded, almost illegible family tree that goes back to a Robert Bulkeley in 1219, just four years after King John of England was forced to sign the Magna Carta. A later Bulkeley is shown to have married a Duchess of York. I know precious little about genealogy, but I do know that the further back you go, the more extravagant the claims get. And hey, we're all descended from Adam and Eve . . . I forge on.

Timeworn as they may be, the family trees come out dueling. Over here are Kilbournes who landed in Connecticut in 1636 and traipsed to Ohio in 1802, eventually becoming inventors, editors, congressmen. Over there are Dennises said to have sailed into Salem, New Jersey, in the 1600s; then there are Egberts who held a land grant in East Jersey from the royal governor and served on the Colonial Council. Down on the Eastern Shore of Maryland were the Tabbses, the Bonds, the MacWilliamses. Some fought in the Revolution. One hobnobbed with Benjamin Franklin. Never mind dubious links to the nobility: It's provenance I'm after now, the better to enhance the value at auction of whatever pieces we can identify.

I sift through everything looking for one Dennis in particular, but, irritatingly, she doesn't turn up on a family tree anywhere. She's Elizabeth Dennis, and she is the maker of a sampler my mother found in a drawer during a great organizing rampage she went on after my dad died. Mother had it framed, and at some point when I was living in New York and feeling far from home, in my early twenties, I simply took it without asking, having no idea at all of its familial or intrinsic value. It survived, and it now hangs in my living room, slowly fading to muted browns and whites. At one point, a neighbor actually made a fresh cross-stitched copy of it.

Who exactly Elizabeth is, I don't know at this point, except that she is clearly one of us. She's a Dennis, we know that. And the date on the sampler—1786—taken together with the 1765 date of Saltar's deed, does bracket the Revolution. As I try to put all of this family information together, the concreteness of the sampler is somehow reassuring. I don't have much to go on at this point, but any proof of a family that might have lived in Philadelphia around the time of the Revolution— better yet, after the Revolution, and in fact the very year before the Constitutional Convention that Washington attended in that city—is another possible connection. The stitching on Elizabeth's sampler is entirely tangible, but I come to think of it as metaphor too: I'm hanging by a thread here, trying to confirm a family claim. I curse the heedlessness with which we as children naturally accepted the claim at face value, and the preoccupation with our own lives later that left us content to keep on accepting it without question.

At the same time, I think wryly of the thread that led through the legendary maze where the Minotaur resided. At least this one is keeping me anchored as I venture into the dusty labyrinth of unexplored family memories that lie behind these documents.

Armed with the sampler and the documents in their faded, ancient handwriting, I set about the task of tracking down more clues to the puzzle: What exactly might some of our ancestors have been doing in colonial Philadelphia, and was there any chance they might have had the opportunity to, um, buy a chair from the Washingtons? A George and Martha yard sale doesn't seem too likely, but the persistence of family legend and a chance name or phrase is after all what took Alex Haley to West Africa in search of Kunta Kinte, and in our family, this chair's appellation was no less mysterious or persistent.

Mother loved history, and as I began to try to reconstruct our family's, I realized what an opportunity we'd missed in Philadelphia. By the time she died, I had worked in and lived outside of the nation's first capital for more than a decade. It's a beautiful city that still retains much of its eighteenth-century skyline, giving it a more human scale than most cities of its size. It is also redolent of American history in a way I'd always found oddly appealing. On my way to my job at the *Inquirer*, I'd drive into the city, over the Ben Franklin Bridge, knowing that the spot where he'd had his print shop was just blocks away. From the top of the bridge I could look down on one of the churches where the Revolution was actually plotted. Coming off the bridge, if traffic wasn't too bad, there was time for a quick glimpse of Independence Hall itself, off to the left across Independence Mall, past the jagged modern sculpture that represents Franklin's legendary lightning bolt.

It was shortly after Daddy's death in the late 1960s that Mother began her campaign to join the Colonial Dames, and perhaps the DAR. As much as anything, I think it was a diversion, a way to cope. The process of establishing her requisite male colonial-era ancestor led to historical ferreting from the Eastern Shore to Indiana—and the aforementioned organizational sweep of the house, which she now had entirely to herself. As I was now discovering, a significant part of the family's history had actually happened in or around Philadelphia, or to people whose roots were there. Yet in all that time, in all her visits to us in South Jersey and her trips with me to the city, except for a casual reference to some ancestor who'd lived in Philly, she never brought it up. She and I actually surfaced at one point from a Philadelphia subway en route to a department store just blocks from where, I'd later realize, one of her great-grandfathers had lived—on South Fifteenth Street, a fashionable area in his time, the 1830s. His address was actually in the family papers—like so much of the information I was now trying to get my head around—and she must have seen that address at some point in looking through them all, but she never mentioned it.

I think perhaps my twentieth-century life in Jersey, which she rather disdained, and the glorious forebears who would be her entrée to the Dames just didn't connect in her mind. Or did she think I wasn't interested? All too likely. Hadn't she, one weekend while I was visiting her in Virginia, given me a box of her family research? And hadn't I handed it back the next morning with some vague comment like, "Well, that was a lot of work"?

As I continue to open the documents, I despair at the missed opportunity. By now I've found Daniel Egbert, that maternal great-grandfather of Mother's, who I've also discovered left Philadelphia to join the Navy shortly after finishing a medical degree at the University of Pennsylvania. His picture always sat in a small gilt frame on the chest of drawers in the living room, so we knew in a vague sort of way that he was important. And we knew his name, but that was about all. He was an Egbert. There were bunches of them, these ancestors. This one had a stiff-looking collar and hair parted on one side. What more would a twentieth-century teenager want to know?

But now here they all are—the Northern Liberties landowner, and Daniel Egbert, who became a ship's doctor, and surely somewhere in here the little girl who in 1786 stitched the fabric that is actually hanging right on my living room wall—and don't I just wish at this moment that Mother was here to help? How could it be that she never told me there were so many of them, whole families of ancestors, living right *here*? How could it be that I never asked?

It seems ironic to me that in a country where people move constantly and so few of us have any idea where we come from, my mother and I might actually have been standing on ground where our family—*our* family—had walked, ridden, danced, talked, eaten, gossiped. Stood there and never spoke of it. Instead, we walked on into Wanamaker's and perhaps bought a scarf or a handbag, and never even thought of them.

Or at least I didn't. I didn't ask the questions that might have elicited the stories, and so, like many of us, I am left with pieces to quilt together with the thread of surmise. We are taught to respect our elders for their age, and to indulge them—imagine!—by listening to their stories. We miss the point utterly, which would be to listen to their tales for what they might tell us of ourselves, and to revere them for creating the fabric of our humanity. Afterward, if they live long enough to see us past the self-absorption of youth, we may come to know them for themselves and to cherish their experiences. But at the outset, we have it exactly backward. In the memories of one's elders is the survival of a part of oneself. We come to that knowledge too late.

※※

WE WEREN'T A FAMILY that saved a lot of letters, and those that remain almost invariably seem chatty and superficial, except for a few plodding accounts of camp life in the War of 1812 that mention who died in some obscure battle. Trust me, I think you had to be there. Most of the photos are unlabeled. The one ancestor who kept a journal spent a lot of time on the weather. That, as it happened, was Daniel Egbert, and of course he was a Navy man, so you can't really blame him. But it's not riveting reading.

I plow through more documents and start visiting historical societies. At least it's a blessing, I think from my South Jersey and Philadelphia vantage point, that the places I need to visit are near where I'm actually living; what would be the odds of that?

Elizabeth Dennis still has me stumped. Though none of the family trees mention her, there is a Caroline Dennis who married Daniel Egbert, he of the boring journal. Daniel is also Harry Clay Egbert's father and my grandmother Bess's grandfather. He seems to have grown up in Philadelphia. In 1837, while at the University of Pennsylvania medical school—I discover in the course of several phone calls to various U of P departmental archives—he wrote a paper on fungi. Riveting.

But there the Philadelphia connection fades. He's off to the Navy, and he never settles down again. First, however, he does marry Caroline Dennis, who will spend most of the rest of her life awaiting his return from sea at various East Coast ports, notably Baltimore.

The Caroline and Daniel connection, though, does have real value in my quest, since he's one of our direct ancestors,

Caroline Dennis

our great-great-grandfather. And that makes Caroline Dennis Egbert, of course, our great-great-grandmother, so while I still may not have any idea how Elizabeth Dennis fits in, I am quite sure it's no accident that we have that sampler, and the date on it is driving me onward. All this for a chair we're hoping to sell for a respectable price at an auction.

One family tree, painstakingly constructed by a long-dead relative my sister vaguely remembers as Aunt Allie,

Daniel Egbert

says that some Dennises landed in the 1600s in Salem, New Jersey. Salem is at the state's southernmost tip, where early sailing vessels from England found safe harbor just across the river from Philadelphia. The city, conveniently, is also located at Exit 1 off the New Jersey Turnpike, on the Delaware Bay, just about an hour south of where I'm living.

Its historical society is open only on weekdays, so I take a day off to drive down.

The docent at the historical society desk treats me with a strained patience bordering on disdain. *People come here all the time looking for their ancestors,* she says. Most of them are clearly deluded, you can read that between her lines—they didn't *really* have ancestors who lived in Salem, poor fools, they just *wish*. But I am quite sure that I did. I have the family documents. I hunt fruitlessly through the card catalog for a couple of hours. Just when it's closing time, I find a bunch of Dennises.

One is a Richard Dennis—a name on Aunt Allie's family tree—but since I didn't have the sense to bring the family stuff along, I can't remember the intertwining threads that brought us all together. But I do remember that Richard Dennis married a Susan Smith, God help us—talk about your needles in a haystack. Mercifully, when I go back and pull out the family trees and look for her and Richard, I see that she comes with a middle name attached: Susan *Salter* Smith. Salter, Saltar. I'm not a genealogist, or I'd know how often in historical and even family records names are misspelled. But I am convinced that I am on the right track, somehow, though who knows why the family thought one woman's middle name was important enough to keep track of—none of the others have middle names. I have to laugh at the ridiculous luck of it all, if this connection pans out. Smith—it must be the commonest name in the English language. Did they anticipate we'd be looking for them all?

Meanwhile, I do have the Elizabeth Dennis sampler, and it is clearly old and authentic, so we know this family tree isn't just a well-meaning figment of someone's imagination, the exasperated woman at the historical society notwithstanding. And weeks later, I have better luck at the Historical Society of Pennsylvania. This time, I take family names and dates with me. I have also, on the advice of someone at the Historical Society with whom I have only spoken by phone, found a document appraiser in North Philadelphia, in the old industrial Bridesburg section, where the first floor of his three-story row house is crammed from floor to ceiling with reference books. He looks over our deeds, tells me how much restorers hate parchment—"it's sheepskin, it's a living thing, it's impossible to work with"—and directs me to an index at the Historical Society that will lead me through the society's publications. If these Dennises and such are to be found anywhere, that'll be the place. He's not too impressed with the deed signed by the Penns, by the way—I guess he's seen a lot of those—but he is very taken with one that has the surname Frank on it, which he says is likely a Jewish family, and much rarer for that period in Philadelphia.

At the Historical Society, an imposing early twentieth-century building in the heart of Philadelphia's historic district, I dutifully stash my purse and everything else except paper and pencil in the outside lockers. I rummage through the card catalog and fill out the little paper slips—one per document—for the reference librarian. After repeated visits to the reference desk and much prowling of the library stacks, I get my answer about our connection to Thomas Saltar of the Northern Liberties, that den of colonial licentiousness. Our Susan Salter Smith, wife of Richard Dennis, is indeed part of Thomas's family, a niece or younger cousin or something. And yes, that middle name is the key that connects us. We've been misspelling it, so make that Susan *Saltar* Smith.

Thomas Saltar, however, is mildly disappointing—no tavern keeper he, nor anything more salacious. Instead, he's a lumber merchant, and while this at first glance doesn't capture my imagination, I do begin to see how following the thread of memory—memories of a family's exploits, but also of its mundane daily life—might bring you to an intersection with history.

I note that Thomas Saltar was ambitious. The library files and stacks reveal that he and his business partners sold their goods to the builders of what might be called Philadelphia's first summer resort—Germantown, up on the heights west of the city. At first a farming village settled by the eponymous German immigrants, it was by the mid-1700s the place where the upper and middle classes retreated to escape the stifling humidity of the seaport city's summers, at the same time avoiding deadly, unexplained outbreaks like the cholera epidemic of 1793.

Saltar, however, didn't simply sell to the elite. He joined them. By 1750, a footnote in one article reveals, he had purchased a house of his own along what is now Germantown Avenue, where just a few years earlier he had been providing the owners of "country seats" with "lumber of various types including scantlings, cedar boards and New England boards" for their mansions.

With the marriage of Susan to Richard, the entrepreneurial Saltars acquired some of the Dennises' cachet, garnered from their having served in the Revolution under General Washington. The now conjoined Saltar-Dennis clan emerges in local historical references as a family with a firm foothold in the upper middle class. In the Pennsylvania Historical Society journals, for instance, I find a diary kept by one Fanny Saltar in the early 1800s. She recalls that her mother's family had a pew near the front of Philadelphia's landmark Christ Church, attending services there with Washington and Franklin; and that her uncle had enjoyed a visit from Thomas Jefferson. One day "when Mr. Jefferson visited my uncle, they walked up to the summerhouse," from which Christ Church, five miles distant, could be seen. Jefferson "looked around and said, This is the spot on which the signers of the Declaration of Independence dined on the day they signed the declaration."

Based on the file cards in Salem, I had assumed Caroline Dennis—daughter of Richard Dennis and Susan Saltar Smith—to be from one of the Quaker families, Salem's earliest settlers, who'd have attended the yearly Quaker meeting in Philadelphia. I'd imagined a dramatic confrontation in which she is written out of the family Bible and forever banished from her family's Quaker meeting and the Society of Friends after announcing that she will marry a military man from Philadelphia, a ship's doctor, who is an Episcopalian to boot.

The facts, when I finally unravel them, are much tamer. She wasn't from Salem at all—the snooty docent was right, I'm chagrined to admit. A handwritten history from Woodbridge, New Jersey, establishes that these Dennises, Richard's branch at least, were from farther north, darn it, and although the document concedes that they came of Quaker stock back in England, they were conveniently Church of England by the time they hit these shores.

It doesn't take an expert to figure out why they might have changed religious loyalties in midstream, as it were. The American Anglicans, after the Revolution, became Episcopalians, abandoning the mother Church of England. But up until the Revolution, being Anglican in New Jersey meant a chance at favors from the Crown's royal governor. For the Dennises of Woodbridge, that would have included land grants, prestige, and a place at the preferred end of the social fabric.

However, I do discover that at least one of these Woodbridge Dennises was both a businessman and a revolutionary, albeit perhaps a somewhat reluctant one. The handwritten history, penned by a member of the Woodbridge Historical Society during the mid-1800s, includes an account of this Dennis's role in the colonists' revolt. It reports that he was the chairman of various committees of protest against the mother country and eventually a delegate to the Provincial Congress as rebellion heated up. After the war, what we hear from him is mainly complaints that he hasn't been reimbursed for the loss of several sloops and a schooner, all loaded with freight, plus "a great store of wine," to the British. Like many supporters of the Revolution, he's now sorely out of pocket, and laments that "he never hath received one farthing as recompense for no part of the same excepting one year's confinement in a loathsome gaol." That was in New York, where the British jailed some of their American prisoners of war, and among his fellow prisoners was Col. Ethan Allen. The prisoners "were often so numerous and so closely packed together," writes his chronicler, "that when they lay on the floor at night, the 'lodgers' could not turn over unless the movement was made by all simultaneously." Their jailer was "a brutal and sordid ruffian" who bragged that he "half-starved 2,000 rebel prisoners." So when one of their fellows was released and sent his old companions "a case of cheese and two cases of porter . . . the persuasive eloquence of stout Ethan Allen, who had a huge frame," induced the hungry inmates to consume the entire windfall in "a magnificent supper at which speeches were made and toasts drank."

❊

I THINK OF HER as coy, this Dennis girl who is ultimately my namesake and who predates Caroline by a generation. Coy, because out of all the embroidery on the sampler, she has left only one bit unfinished, and that's the one that would have told us her age:

Elizabeth Dennis is my
name I was _____ years old
when I wrought the
same In the year of our
Lord 1786

On the other hand, I think, perhaps she was merely practical, leaving the age till last lest it change before she finished the sampler. Or perhaps she died from one of those sudden, sweeping childhood epidemics that routinely decimated communities, like the fabled fever that stalked Philadelphia in summertime and sent inhabitants who could afford it scurrying for the heights of Germantown, where the air was clear and cooler. But I like to think that she demurely skipped the stitches that would have completed the work—an 8, perhaps, or 11?—leaving her audience forever unable to complete the math and capture the fact of her advancing age.

By now my quest for the provenance of the alleged Washington chair has taken me to Independence National Historic Park, where I'd done the research for the bicentennial of the Constitution back in 1987. It occurs to me to call their library, where I have a contact, and ask for help. The park extends over the footprint of the house where the Washingtons lived during his presidency. Would they have any record of the furniture? Email us a photo, they tell me.

The INHP staff are cordial and accommodating, and soon I am talking with two archivists and a furniture expert. *Well,*

A family sampler would lead into a labyrinth of clues.

they inform me, *we know that George Washington did buy some French furniture, and this piece of yours certainly could be that old. But it doesn't look like anything we have records of. That doesn't say it's not his chair, but it isn't one we can identify.*

Drat. Back to the drawing board. The date on the sampler is the thread I am still following as I try to reason through this puzzle.

Samplers (from the Latin *exemplar*) were intended to show a young girl's deftness at handwork, a crucial talent for any homemaker-in-training in the days before sewing machines. A sampler by custom was "signed" and dated. A simple sampler might be sewn by a girl of five or six, a more complicated one by a child of ten or twelve. By her teen years, a young woman would have proven her skill at samplers and moved on to more complicated tasks such as helping sew the family's wardrobe.

Piecing the Saltars and Dennises together, I finally conclude Elizabeth must have been my great-great-grandmother Caroline's aunt. The date on the sampler puts Elizabeth in the same generation as Richard, Caroline's father; she would have been his younger sister.

And given the date—1786—I try to deduce her age and her place in the family. She'd likely have been too young to have any memory of the Revolution itself, but she would have grown up in the era of the Philadelphia that knew George Washington as a visitor during the dramatic days of the first Constitutional Convention in 1787, the city that claimed him as a resident after it became the U.S. capital in 1790.

If she were of an age to be stitching samplers in 1786, she would have been a young woman during his Philadelphia years, when he posed for the famous Gilbert Stuart portrait in 1796. Perhaps, if she lived to marry and set up housekeeping, she might have gone with her sister-in-law—Susan Saltar Smith Dennis, Caroline's mother—to a prestigious auction where some interesting household goods were for sale.

Having lived for some twenty years in the Philadelphia area by this time, I know that at one point the Washingtons lived in a house belonging to Robert Morris, the renowned financier of the American Revolution. I also remember that after the war, Morris's finances took a turn for the worse. A quick bout of sleuthing on the Web sends me to several general reference books, which confirm that Morris was imprisoned for debt from 1798 to 1801, when Congress actually changed the bankruptcy laws in part to release him. His slide to ruin, fueled largely by land speculation, would have started much sooner. By the time the Washingtons left town, he could have been forced to forfeit whatever goods remained in his possession.

But before his downfall, the Morris mansion he lent to the Washingtons was deemed the finest house in the city. The Washingtons, I learn, also spent time in another home belonging to Morris, up in Germantown, where the ambitious Saltars would by then have become an established part of resort society. If any furniture the Washingtons left behind was going to be auctioned, either for the retiring president or perhaps for Morris's creditors, the Saltars would certainly not have missed the opportunity to grab a bit of the great man's legacy.

Again, the Historical Society of Pennsylvania comes to the rescue. At two A.M. one night, when I've been wrestling with what I know about Robert Morris, George Washington, the Dennises, Philadelphia in the 1790s, and a bunch of other stuff, I somewhat wearily go back to their website. Idly I type in "Robert Morris George Washington chairs auction" and I hit pay dirt: an article about Robert Morris's homes in Philadelphia that includes a newspaper advertisement from 1797. It's for a public auction scheduled at the Morris mansion on Market Street, which had come to be called the President's House:

> Sales of Elegant Furniture,
> On Friday Next the 10th instant, at 1 o'clock,
> will be sold by public Auction, at the House of
> the late President of the United States,
> in Market street,
> A QUANTITY
> of Valuable Household
> FU RN I T U R E,
> belonging to General Wash-
> ington, among which are, a number of Elegant
> Chairs with Sattin Bottoms, sattin Window
> Curtains, a Beautiful Cut Glass Lustre, and a very
> complete Mahogany Writing Desk, also,
> a Coach and Phaeton.
> Footman & Co. auctioneers

Was *our* GW chair of family legend one of these with elegant "Sattin Bottoms"? It could have occupied the townhome or the Germantown country house, which Independence National Historic Park archives call the oldest surviving U.S. presidential home, a house where Washington held state dinners and cabinet meetings. A chair in which George Washington might once have *sat*—or in which at least someone *conversing* with George Washington would certainly have sat . . .

It's the sort of thing my mother would have loved. And we could have shared it, she and I. Perhaps it would have led us through the papers together. Perhaps we'd have patched together a connection with the ancestors scattered in burial plots across the country and beyond. We might have healed a little of the loss that comes of never having had a permanent home, or even have spoken of who we really were and why we left so many things unsaid.

The George Washington chair

On the day we came up the stairs from the Market-Frankford subway in Philadelphia, steps that smelled of soot and stale urine the way the steps from subways do, Mother was telling me that she was sure that if her father had been home with the family the winter Little Brother caught pneumonia, her young Down syndrome brother would have lived. She recalled how when she had polio, her father had sat by her bedside for days, rubbed her legs, and all but willed her to heal. And she grew up to walk without a trace of a limp. But that year, Charlie had already gone ahead to the Philippines, where the rest of the family was to join him, and Little Brother died, to be remembered at last by name on a tombstone in Arlington, youngest of the Kilbourne children.

We are haunted by lost opportunity, my mother and I. Perhaps I could get interested in genealogy after all. It could, I'm beginning to see, be sort of like sweeping the beach with one of those metal detectors. You never know when you might uncover someone's lost engagement ring—or the answer to a family riddle.

Meanwhile, despite the tantalizing discovery of the Washingtons' Market Street auction, my research on our chair's provenance has not yielded up that definitive connection—the eighteenth-century bill of sale, as it were—and the auction is almost upon us. The catalog will allude to George Washington, but without a definitive claim about the chair. It will have to stand on its own merits.

Chapter 7

ALMOST FAMOUS: THE PISTOLS AND THE RED CHAIR

BY EARLY FALL, THE AUCTION DATE WAS SET FOR JANUARY. But while Sam, the appraiser, was probing the furniture for its likely value, we already knew that not all of the items she was evaluating would go on the block. While I'd been sifting through the documents Sam had discovered and combing through the files of historical societies on the Philadelphia end, Jeanne had located the typed lists that indicated which pieces of furniture belonged to her and which to me.

The lists were from a day sometime back in the 1980s, from a divvying up we'd done over a weekend on one of the rare occasions when we were both home visiting Mother at the same time. Our mother, as you might not be surprised to hear, was not one to let the grass grow under her feet. She too was the child of highly effective people, and a child of the military to boot, and when she had a plan, she wasted no time in implementing it. On this particular afternoon, I think Jeanne and I were lounging around unsuspectingly after lunch when she pounced.

Pouncing after a meal was one of Mother's specialties. Jeanne and I often surmised that it was a reflex ingrained by her years of training in how to deal considerately with the servants. And those years would have comprised most of her life, with the exception of two bleak periods when she and Daddy couldn't afford to have servants, during his early years stateside in the Army, and right after World War II, when he'd retired from the service. The rest of the time, she'd have been operating under the assumption, learned at her mother's table, that you don't dawdle once the meal is done. You might withdraw to the sitting room for coffee or cordials, but you would not linger in the dining room when the help needed to clear the table and get on with the dishes.

In the real world where Jeanne and I, conversely, had spent most of our lives, the help who'd be washing the dishes were precisely the same ones who'd fixed the meal, and that would be ourselves; and if there was a moment of leisure to be seized at the table over a cup of coffee at the end of a meal, we would seize it. This led to an ongoing tug-of-war whenever we visited Mother—who by now, living alone, had installed a dishwasher and was doing her own cooking and cleaning, but still honored the now-vanished servants. We'd finish the meal and prepare to lounge. She'd exclaim, "Well!"—which, as Miss Manners has pointed out, is the signal by host or guest that the social event is about to conclude—leap up from the table, and start clearing the dishes.

And so it happened, on that afternoon, that we found ourselves herded to the living room, where she parked us and told us to draw straws. She'd said for years that this was how we would do it: We'd draw straws one day, and we'd take turns choosing items we wanted to keep, one at a time. By now she was in her seventies, and quite cognizant of the fact that her daughters didn't often show up at her house at the same time. She was on a mission. "I don't want you girls fighting over things after I'm gone," she said brightly, handed us two broom straws, and left the room.

So we drew straws and started the penultimate winnowing of the furniture, the chairs and portraits, rugs and tables and lamps and clutter we'd someday inherit. I got the long straw and immediately took the Chippendale sofa on which we were sitting. *Ha!* Jeanne coolly claimed the beautiful butler's table in front of it, which Mother had told us a soldier at some post had handmade for our grandfather Joe Tracy—Daddy's father. *Rats, I'd wanted that.* I took the table made from the brass tray that Charlie and Bessie had acquired somewhere in their postings abroad. Jeanne put her name on the portrait of Adm. William Maxwell Wood that had hung over the Empire sofa in our grandmother Jeanne's apartment in Washington. The process was nerve-racking, even for two sisters who had for most of our lives functioned as long-distance best friends. Put yourself in our place: You're dividing up treasures garnered over many lifetimes, which are also the essence of your childhood home. But actually, you don't want to divide it at all; you want it to stay exactly where it is. You don't ever want to see it any way other than the way it has always been. And you're doing this with your best friend. Scalpel, please!

Fast-forward. It's 2002, and we are now beginning the final triage of this household, which up until now, through its various moves under our watch, has been divided only in theory. We're on the phone long distance, Jeanne and I. In retrospect, it was lucky she'd taken notes that day and had the presence of mind to type and file them. They'd anchor us as we decided what to relinquish and what we couldn't bear to let go of.

She's snail-mailed me a copy of the lists, since they were written and typed—unbelievable as it now seems—before either of us even knew there was an Internet. We start picking through them, one item at a time, attempting to balance how much each of us is contributing to the auction pile.

If we were going to bother to have an auction, we'd already agreed, we'd have to include some of the best stuff, treasures that would surely draw a good crowd of appreciative, eager buyers.

So, like it or not, we are weighing the need to provide valuable stuff for the auction against our attachment to the individual objects. The lists are essential, since Jeanne is in upstate New York, I'm in New Jersey, and Sam and all the furniture are in Virginia. We're deciding what goes and what stays, working from memory (we have plenty of that) and from the inventory Jeanne typed after that day in the living room.

As we go through the lists, we earmark some of the easier items first. Jeanne will contribute the Empire sofa, with its uncomfortably plump gold upholstery; the Federal armchair; the rosewood lady's parlor chair. I'll give up the Canton china, including the tall *famille verte* vase made into a lamp; the George Washington chair; the elaborately carved Victorian cherrywood vanity; and the vast mahogany dining room set whose table, instead of having removable leaves, slid apart into four separate pieces—just try to find a place to store *those* when you're not using them.

Not so easy, for Jeanne, is the little black desk with the brass handles and the secret side panel that opened to reveal drawers. As girls we'd both been enchanted by its magical compartments, but it was supremely impractical—you had to

pull out the long flat drawer across the front before you could
open the foldout desktop, or else its brass hinges would break.
They'd already been mended once.

As for me, I wince at the very thought of sacrificing the
sandai chest and the Chinese tapestry, which hung for decades

The Empire sofa

on the dining room wall behind the chest. But we think both
might be museum pieces, with the added possible interest of
having been brought back by our grandfather from the Boxer
Rebellion. The chest is beautiful, the luster of its highly polished wood like a fire under the surface. And at one point
Mother years earlier had gotten a very interesting appraisal of
the tapestry from a Chinese watercolorist who'd happened to
be teaching at one of the local colleges. But his assessment
would turn out to be just one piece of hoped-for provenance
that would get lost, perhaps literally, in translation.

Provenance was foremost in our minds, as per Sam's instruction, as we went down the lists. In *The Lure of the Antique*, turn-of-the-century antiquarian Walter Dyer wrote, "It seems to me there are two parts to this question of the truth about antique furniture. Is the antiquity of a piece of furniture genuine? If so, what is the old thing good for, anyway?"

As Dyer notes, one of the things that helps sell an antique is its authenticity. Another—failing, as Dyer pointed out, usefulness—is its having belonged to somebody or someplace important. In the world of antiques, provenance ideally speaks of both.

For us—as Dyer so cogently inquired—the continuing question was, what *is* the old thing good for, anyway? Why would anyone buy this stuff, and how could we make it as desirable as possible? I think we were looking for validation as much as money. In fact, maybe even more so. Validation of the forebears who were not only ultimately responsible for producing us, but had also equipped us with all this furniture they obviously thought was worthwhile enough to transport over oceans and continents—and to pass down to descendants they'd never meet, to own and enjoy.

So: These ancestors, about whom the documents had started to give us at least some idea—could they be of any help in unloading their belongings for a price that would do those possessions justice? In my imagination, the history the pieces carried with them spoke for itself. Spoke? It *shouted* the story of how we came to be here—not just our family, but the country, the nation that this family had served so long and so unquestioningly, in so many times and places. And all for what? So that we could sell the most tangible proof of that history to a bunch of strangers and stop paying the bill for a couple of storage bins? My guilt sometimes began to get the better of me as I wondered whether I was betraying my family and their contributions to that history.

But their prominence was perhaps just in my imagination, filled as it was with stories our buyers would probably never hear, about the Philadelphia lumber merchant and the Navy officers, about our grandparents and the times they knew. They were interesting enough people, perhaps, but not celebrities. I had to acknowledge that if a certain Empire chest of drawers had come down in Douglas MacArthur's family instead of his comrade-at-arms Charlie Kilbourne's, its history wouldn't have died with its sale.

Of course, we did have that chair with the tantalizing story of its potentially distinguished provenance. If we could have definitively proven that it had been sat in by George Washington, its story—to say nothing of its monetary value—would only have grown over time.

These and other illustrious names lurked in our family's background, as did various heroic deeds that had certainly made headlines at the time—like Harry Egbert's death—but had since receded, most annoyingly, into the vast swamp of history without leaving a trace worth talking about—or trading upon, as we were hoping to do in this auction.

It was Harry, after all, who had fallen while leading the charge at San Juan Hill, but Teddy Roosevelt who had claimed the day and seized the credit. And there was William Maxwell Wood Sr., the uniformed naval officer in the portrait and Daddy's great-grandfather, for whom he was named. This Wood, first of two by that name who'd been naval officers, sailed against the pirates of the Caribbean, quite literally, and against slave traders off the Brazil coast before becoming Surgeon of the Pacific Fleet around 1844. At the outset of the Mexican War in 1846, he happened to be crossing Mexico and—posing in civilian clothes as an English gentleman—did some intelligence work that his commander, Commodore Sloat, later credited with enabling the United States to claim California as a territory. Wood accompanied Admiral Perry on the mission that opened trade with Japan in the 1850s, met the King of Siam (of *King and I* fame), and later wrote *Fankwei* (*Foreign Devil*) about the Second Opium War in China. But at the same time, Wood *wasn't* Perry. So, cancel any name-associated value that would accrue to any pieces that might have belonged to him. Minus celebrity, they're just another bunch of antiques.

Then there was Charles Erskine Wood—"crazy Cousin Ernie," as various family members called him, perhaps because in later life he was a self-proclaimed anarchist with wild hair who wrote poetry. The second son of the aforementioned William Maxwell Wood Sr., he had ridden with the cavalry in 1877 in pursuit of the great Nez Perce leader Chief Joseph, and it was Charles Erskine Wood who took notes as the translator rendered the chief's famous surrender speech: *From where the sun now stands, I will fight no more forever.* Afterward, Erskine Wood was ordered to escort Chief Joseph to the nearby Army camp where his captivity would officially begin. "I nodded pleasantly to the chief and tried to look, at least, as if it were all friendly," he wrote later. Still later, his son spent a summer living on the reservation with Chief Joseph's family. But of course Charles Erskine wasn't Chief Joseph or even a member of his tribe; he was just a bystander in history who'd happened to write down the famous speech.

And it was pretty much the same for all the rest of them—like James Kilbourne, for instance, who set forth from Massachusetts as a teenager at the end of the Revolutionary War, which had claimed the lives of several family members and left the family farm in ruins. Eventually, he'd cofound a town in Ohio, fight in the War of 1812, serve in Congress, and propose a bill that would someday become the basis of the Homestead Act; and he'd go bankrupt at least once, when he overstepped himself trying to establish a commercial empire in central Ohio. But who really remembers, or would care?

A photo from 1868 shows several members of the Kilbourne family in Wyoming, on a barnstorming tour with presidential candidate Ulysses S. Grant and Gen. William Tecumseh Sherman—another familial brush with history; some Kilbourne was an influential supporter of Grant in some way that not even the family now remembers, but there they all are, out in Wyoming at a railroad station somewhere with the candidate. And then there was Sen. Joseph Rodman West, a member of Congress from Louisiana whose house in a tony neighborhood off Massachusetts Avenue made him a neighbor of General Sherman in 1870, according to the U.S. census for that year. This is another obscure bit of history I uncover while sorting through the documents, and again it doesn't help bolster the value of the furniture. But it does set me thinking again about how things get handed down, and from whom. And it also represents what I came to describe, with a certain grim humor, as the perils of being almost famous.

❧

A PAIR OF OLD PISTOLS were the perfect example of that phenomenon, and their almost-famousness was in the end part of what saved them from going under Bill Harlowe's gavel. They also illustrate something about the way stories get handed down in a family, and with the stories, provenance—or at least a shot at it.

As Mother began delving into family history, she concentrated on her side of the family. Of course, this made perfectly practical sense: That was the side that was germane to proving her Colonial Dame–worthiness; it was also the side she knew best—and the side with whose stories we'd grown up, living in Charlie's house.

We did subliminally gather from her, however, that my grandmother Jeanne's family, the Wests and the Woods, were rather aristocratic as American families went. Mother might not have felt very close to her mother-in-law, but she did hang the portrait of Admiral Wood in the living room, over the Kilbournes' Chippendale sofa, and she did mention crazy Cousin Ernie and show us his picture, with the wild hair and beard—but it wasn't until years later that a cousin from Daddy's side of the family told us his story.

About Daddy's father's family—the Tracys and Powells and their forebears—we knew even less. There was some story about someone's having lost all his money in the crash of 1929, and it always had a vaguely disreputable sound to it, as if he had been in, well, the trades, or banking, or something. Mother somehow seemed not to have gotten around to investigating that end of the family. Nor had she given much shrift to her mother-in-law's furniture except for a couple of the really nice smaller pieces, such as the rosewood love seat and lady's parlor chair, or something as undeniably useful as the highboy she stored linens in. But as for their stories, these pieces weren't asked to speak, at least not in Mother's house. Pretty as they were, they were to be seen and not heard.

There was one exception: a pair of old wooden dueling pistols Daddy and Mother had brought back from his mother's apartment during that expedition to Washington after Big Jeanne's death.

The pistols. Jeanne and I had been completely unaware of their existence until the afternoon Mother revealed them to me, sometime after she and Daddy came back from that Washington triage. That was the day she unveiled—with a dramatic flourish and a grave air of secrecy—our ownership of, ahem, the so-called Aaron Burr pistols.

I was in high school at the time and Jeanne was on a Fulbright in Germany. Mother said she had something to show me and led me to what had been Jeanne's room and was now a guest room. We knelt together in front of the low carved wooden toy chest Daddy had made for Jeanne when she was just a baby. And so for one of the very few times in our young lives, with Jeanne away, I as the younger sister actually got first crack at a family revelation.

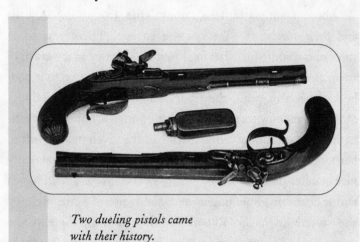

Two dueling pistols came
with their history.

With ceremony, Mother lifted the lid of the old toy chest and reached in to retrieve a plain but handsome walnut wood case with a brass handle that folded into its top when not in use. Opening it, she revealed the two pistols, lying snugly facing in opposite directions.

In the afternoon light under the window where we knelt beside the chest, Mother lifted one out, very carefully, and turned it in her hand. Its stock was exquisitely polished walnut with carbon steel fittings. It is unusual, I would read later, to find dueling pistols without a lot of fancy engraving and "extra fancy wood." These were plain, with ornamentation so subtle you'd miss it at first glance.

Pistols—would it even be legal to have them in your house? These pistols, moreover, were valuable, as Mother was now about to reveal to me. It seemed the pistols had been a shared secret among the grown-ups—just one of the many secrets, to be sure, the grown-ups kept from us, as grown-ups routinely do. But these were pistols!

And how exactly did the pistols come into Daddy's family? We didn't even get to that question; I am sure I was too stunned that afternoon to ask, because what Mother was about to tell me was that these pistols—*these* pistols—had belonged to Aaron Burr.

She would hasten to say that they were not—we were not claiming that they were—*the* Aaron Burr pistols. Not the ones that attended the fatal duel with Alexander Hamilton above the banks of the Hudson River. But they were, somehow, pistols that at some time had belonged to Burr. And they had come into our family somewhere along the way.

The family documents and a visit to a cemetery in upstate Pennsylvania would eventually help a little in the question of our place in the Burr saga, giving us the name Burr Tracy and thus at least a putative connection, but unfortunately not until after Mother and Daddy were both dead—leaving us once again with no one to ask.

⁂

THE LATE 1700S AND early 1800s have been called the "golden age" of dueling with pistols. To have a pair of dueling pistols in your house was to proclaim your position as a gentleman, a man of honor who moreover was entitled to defend that honor. They were a status symbol, an emblem of your place among the upper classes. Among notables known to have taken up pistols in an affair of honor were Stephen Decatur (killed in a duel) and Andrew Jackson (said to have fought at least a dozen and perhaps as many as a hundred). And in America at least, the most famous duel of all was the one with Burr that cost Hamilton his life.

Burr and Hamilton had been personal and political enemies for more than a decade when they finally met with pistols and seconds—as the result of a remark Hamilton had made about Burr at a political dinner—below the Palisades in Weehawken, New Jersey, on a July morning in 1804. Hamilton is said to have fired the first shot, into the air. Burr fired second, his bullet tearing through Hamilton's abdomen, liver, and diaphragm. Hamilton died the next day.

Toward the end of his life, Burr reportedly said he "should have known the world was wide enough for Hamilton and me." In the two centuries since, history has variously judged the event. Overall, Burr—who was charged with murder but never convicted—has come down as the villain of the piece, a man John Adams considered "unprincipled" and whom

Thomas Jefferson called "a crooked gun . . . a great man in little things, really small in great ones."

"*Not* the ones he shot Alexander Hamilton with, of *course,*" Mother would say. Of course not, indeed. I didn't ask how she knew that, but of course a historically respectable family wouldn't dream of harboring a murder weapon. Moreover, a famous murder weapon would have its provenance very well established and would be residing in a museum somewhere and not in some family's attic. It would not be merely *almost* famous.

What the pistols would accomplish for Jeanne and me was to propel us on a search for the Burrs in our family. One of the few scraps of information that had been handed down about Daddy's side of the family was that they'd come to Washington from Towanda, Pennsylvania—an old factory town in the Endless Mountains overlooking the Susquehanna River— sometime before the Crash of 1929. That date was fixed in family memory because they'd supposedly lost a lot of money in the crash. Looking at a map, Jeanne and I discovered that Towanda wasn't far across the state border from her home in Binghamton. I drove up from Philadelphia, and she took a day off from work so we could hit the Towanda Historical Society, which we'd located online, when it was open for visitors. In their files, we discovered none other than one Burr Tracy. We excitedly set off to troll the town's cemeteries, searching three before finally finding Burr and his family up on Oak Hill.

From Towanda—as I learned from subsequent digging in the Washington, D.C., public library's microfiches—Burr Tracy found his way to Washington, where newspaper records show he was embroiled in a real estate scandal in the 1890s. He then vanishes from the public record—eventually to end up

back in Towanda, up on Oak Hill—but not before making sure
his son Joe, our paternal grandfather, was awarded a coveted
entrance to West Point, the U.S. Military Academy, and thus to
the officers' ranks. Joe Tracy's path through the Army would
be the essential opposite of Charlie Kilbourne's, devoid of
spectacular deeds, stories, and medals, but Joe would eventually
become a brigadier general—no small feat over a lifetime spent
mostly in the peacetime Army. And he would marry Jeanne
West Wood, and pass on a pair of beautifully made pistols with
the Burr legend attached. Besides their intrinsic beauty, the pistols would certainly have had some value on the auction block
as antique firearms. But they were among the objects we decided to keep, because without anyone in the family left to ask,
there was no way to figure out whether we had a real connection to the infamous duelist. And without provenance, what
they'd bring as just another nice pair of antiques wasn't com-
mensurate to their value as a great family story.

If only they had been *those* pistols . . . but they weren't.

WE JUST COULDN'T bring ourselves to let go of what were
probably some of the best pieces. The Canton china and the
Washington chair (mine) were both too delicate and too valuable for our assessment of our competence as caretakers—no
problem there. But the pistols (Jeanne's) were just too beautiful and interesting to part with, and though old and in need of
careful handling, they didn't take up much space. They could
be tucked away in their case, which after all had preserved
them for more than two centuries now.

Among the other things we just couldn't bring ourselves to
part with were the beautiful mahogany butler's table (Jeanne's)

and the Egbert rocker (ditto). The Chippendale sofa (mine) was certainly not convenient when it came to storing and moving, but it had really been Mother's favorite spot. And the red chair (also mine) had been Charlie's.

In the realm of the famous—or almost—Charlie had probably the best shot of all the family at stardom, at least in military circles. His father, a West Point graduate, was attached to the Signal Department and Weather Bureau. Charlie was born at Fort Whipple, Virginia, now Fort Myers, and spent his boyhood there and in nearby Washington, where Ulysses S. Grant was passing his time not distinguishing himself as president. Charlie's father was the career officer and military science instructor; his mother, Ada, a Coolidge of San Francisco. She probably hated Ohio, where—after Washington—the family would spend the balance of Charlie's youth. Charlie left Ohio for the Virginia Military Institute and entered the U.S. Signal Corps, the post that took him to the Philippines as a wartime volunteer.

It's not clear what propelled this son of a peacetime army to become one of the most decorated soldiers of his era. In *An Army Boy in Pekin,* he describes the reckless spirit that lingered with him even in old age: "A wild excitement, in keeping with his surroundings, took possession of the young American. All sense of personal danger left him. He did not know whether he could get through, and somehow, he did not seem to care." Yet in an interview in 1937 he describes World War I as a "filthy war," and—in a voice probably intended for the young men he was by then leading at VMI—cautions that war is never otherwise and that it is folly to be seduced by thoughts of glory. "You had to live underground, and the underground beasts came to live with you. All night long in the trenches you could hear them squeaking. And there was nothing to relieve the sordidness." He describes the "thirty minutes of waiting just before going over the top to face death," when "a man thinks of himself." Men who know war, he says, "do not want it." At around the same time, in the 1930s, he advised a nephew who was also his namesake not to join the Army for yet another reason: In contrast to the grim reality of war, he pointed out, was the tedious reality of peace. He'd just spent the final fifteen years of his career amid the politicking peacetime Army, and it must have seemed a supreme exercise in futility.

For the first half of his military life, however, he saw little enough of that tedium. His entrée to the U.S. Army, where he fought those three early wars in quick succession, was followed by several years stateside. But it seemed his fortunes lay in the Philippines, or perhaps he thought they did because of his first spectacular success there. When the Army announced its intention to fortify the strategic island of Corregidor in Manila Bay—gateway to the island nation's capital—he requested a transfer and was granted command of the operation that would dismantle the ornate old Spanish cannons and install, in 1909, then state of the art guns on the island's hilly terrain. Neither he nor the U.S. high command had any way of knowing then that decades later, in World War II, Charlie's once formidable gunnery would still be the island's principal defense when the Japanese attacked the islands.

World War I took him to France, where he earned the nation's two highest honors besides the Medal of Honor—the Distinguished Service Cross and the Distinguished Service Medal—as well as the French Croix de Guerre and Légion d'Honneur, making him the Army's most decorated soldier of the era. But the Philippines continued to draw him back. William Manchester, in his biography of Douglas MacArthur, writes of how the general and others were caught under the spell of what MacArthur called "the blue." The deep, lingering Pacific twilights wrapped Manila—where both MacArthur and Charlie were repeatedly stationed—in an almost midnight blue as day faded off toward the Asian mainland, and from Charlie's writings about the Philippines, it is evident he was under the same spell. His final gesture toward the islands where he had fought and married, seen the births of his first three children, and witnessed the deaths of many comrades— the islands that were as close to a home as any place he'd known until then—was a fortification.

When he attended the Army War College, the Army's top center for strategic training, in 1920, the theme for the year was how to forestall or defeat an anticipated Japanese conquest of the Pacific—surprisingly, in retrospect, given that world attention for the preceding five years had been focused on a world war fought primarily in Europe. Charlie later wrote that he had never lost sight of that year's instruction. He and Bessie were stationed in the Philippines a total of five times, and on their last posting there, in the early 1930s, he finally had the chance to put into action the ideas he'd developed about the perceived Japanese threat.

Under the treaty regulations of the time, his plan for the underground fortification that would go down in history as the Malinta Tunnel was not billed as such. An American-Japanese agreement in 1922 had forbidden the arming of the islands of the Western Pacific. The Japanese ignored and defied the order on the islands they controlled, including Guam, but between fidelity to the treaty and a reluctance to spend money on arms in peacetime, the United States offered no funding for building defenses in their remote Philippine territory. A plan to build a munitions storage bunker in the Malinta Hill was broached by the Harbor Defense commander under the guise of a public works project in 1922, but little came of it. The real development of the warren of tunnels had to await the return of the officer who had installed the first of Corregidor's twentieth-century guns in 1909.

In their book *Corregidor: The Saga of a Fortress,* James H. and William M. Belote describe it thus: "Although the improvement of Corregidor's defenses seemed an impossibility, three remarkable officers refused to adopt a do-nothing policy, and risked their careers to tackle the Rock's most vexing problem, bombardment from Bataan. Shortly after World War I, a Harbor Defense commander had proposed emplacing a secure headquarters and storage area under Malinta Hill. In 1931 Brigadier General Charles E. Kilbourne blandly announced in a routine dispatch his intention of constructing a 'tunnel road' through the hill for the convenience of the Air Corps garrison at Kindley Field. Covered by Major General John Gulick, who permitted no discussion of the true nature of the project at Coast Artillery Headquarters, Kilbourne used his post's maintenance allowance to begin construction, employing old mining equipment and prison labor. His friend and successor, Brigadier General Stanley D. Embick, continued the task, lining the main corridor and laterals with concrete and laying out the north and south supplemental storage areas. Work went on until the system was substantially completed in 1938" (pp. 34–35).

By 1932 it was an open secret in military and some government circles that the corridors under the old Spanish battlements could accommodate tons of munitions and emergency supplies and sustain several thousand troops for an estimated six months—the time Charlie reckoned would be needed for the U.S. Navy to arrive to lift a naval siege. Though the underground citadel is remembered as the Malinta Tunnel, to think of it as a single tunnel is to greatly underestimate the enormous scale of the undertaking. In a letter he wrote after his farewell visit there in 1954, Charlie casually mentions that besides the arms and ammunition, some half a million tons of beef had been stored in freezers in the side tunnels, which also included a hospital, war rooms, and living quarters—a whole city underground, with a steady supply of fresh water from a well deep in the hill. This was the tunnel that would shelter Douglas MacArthur and thousands of his shattered forces, along with the Philippine government, after the Japanese invaded the Philippine archipelago at the end of 1941.

William Manchester, in *American Caesar*, recalls the terror of that time: "Manila had no sooner been proclaimed an open city than Mitsubishis bombed it, razing the old church of Santo Domingo, the college of San Juan de Latran, and the Philippine Herald. . . . Seizing the capital, [Japanese general Masaharu] Homma announced that natives who were unenthusiastic about the occupation would be confined in concentration camps or beheaded." As the beleaguered American and Filipino forces retreated down the Bataan Peninsula, MacArthur evacuated several thousand troops, Filipino officials, and American civilians including his own wife and son to Corregidor.

The tunnels built under Charlie's command in the early 1930s held MacArthur and his men and provided hospital space and a fortress from which to fight back as best they could until at last the general and his party were smuggled out, vowing to return. The guns that Charlie had installed during that much earlier tour of duty, in 1909, would provide the main defense for the troops in the tunnels and in foxholes who held off the Japanese for a total of five months.

MacArthur's reconquest of the islands is the stuff of both history and legend. Charlie's Malinta defenses may have saved the only general who had the sheer reckless courage to defeat the Japanese. After the war, a British assessment of the war in the Pacific reported that those five months probably cost Japan its plan to invade Australia. They also bought MacArthur the time for his initial escape from the islands and delayed the Japanese in their intended conquest of the Pacific long enough to enable MacArthur's return.

Charlie retired from the Army in 1936, just before the completion of the Malinta Tunnel. The tunnel was surely the culmination of his life as a fighter and a strategist—as well as an engineer—for he was that too, by his education and training at VMI. It must have seemed ironic to him, in retrospect, to have lived so long in the Army only to retire as the greatest war of his cohort's lifetime was about to begin. He and Bessie would be safely on the sidelines in the superintendent's quarters at VMI—a blessing, objectively, given his age and the horrors endured by Americans who remained in Manila and their Filipino counterparts. But he must have found it hard to sit it out.

❦

MY GRANDFATHER'S RED CHAIR was one of the few things I took home with me to New Jersey after Mother died. There it sat in my living room, and behind it, like an aide-de-camp, the lacquered tip-top table, in the spot it would have occupied in my grandparents' house. The chair is mid- to late nineteenth century, perhaps mahogany, its dark wood carved with the flourishes the Victorians were so fond of. Its shape suited him well; it was clearly a gentleman's chair, its seat high enough off the ground to accommodate long legs, its arms at just the height for an elbow to rest comfortably, almost regally, at ease. Its high back seemed to mimic my grandfather's slender frame—the narrow waist flaring into broader but elegant shoulders, a physique that carried a uniform well. The chair back is crowned with a rococo swirl, and it draws itself up from its scrolled feet to its topknot in an almost thronelike way.

The red chair occupied its corner of my grandparents' living room with a subtle feng shui, its back firmly against a jutting corner where the bay window met the rest of the room. It was a command post, the bay window overlooking the yard and street corner in one direction, its occupant facing the double front doors across the living room in the other. In my New Jersey living room, I noticed, the chair sat almost invariably empty, save for an occasional guest who failed to perceive that it was already occupied. It's not that I actually imagined *he* was there, of course . . . it was just the habit of memory that conjured him in his customary whites—the crisply ironed linen pants, the finely woven short-sleeved shirts—smoking one of his long, unfiltered cigarettes on those long, cool summer mornings of my childhood.

The shirts and handkerchiefs came from the Philippines, along with the cigarettes and the endless stream of little presents—straw slippers, beaded boxes, wooden toys for his grandchildren. The gifts were sent by Filipino admirers, families of men who had fought first alongside, then against, and then once more as allies of the Americans in the bewildering whirlwind of their nation's twentieth-century history. The little gifts and the essential smokes continued after his last visit, in the mid-1950s, to the city he so loved. A picture shows him in Manila in his white linen suit, standing with cadets of the Philippine Constabulary he'd helped establish, the young men listening politely to the old warrior from America whose battles had helped shape the military careers they were now beginning.

Toward the end of his life, my grandfather would refer to the United States' expropriation of the Philippines as perhaps its most unblemished and noble military undertaking—almost the identical terms MacArthur applied to the post–World War II reconstruction of Japan. Subsequent history, it may be argued, proved the U.S. role less salutary; Charlie lived to revisit the scenes of his young manhood, but not to see the ascension of the Marcos family.

I see him in the rising heat of a summer day, sitting in the red chair, awaiting a visitor. There were many in those days of his eighties, a scant decade after the end of the Second World War. For him and his lifelong comrades-at-arms, it was a time of ease tinged with poignancy. They could visit one another freely and at length, bringing their wives with them. The wars they had fought as young men, risking their lives, and those of later years in which they'd borne the awful responsibility for other young men's lives, were behind them. Ahead, however, the only certainty was of growing older, of "fading away," as MacArthur put it, and eventually—MacArthur's demurral notwithstanding—of death. There is an elegant melancholy to their meetings in the parlor, its windows shuttered against the heat.

An occasional visitor was a younger man named Frank McCarthy, himself a VMI graduate who'd been an aide to Gen. George Marshall during World War II. Even as a child I always knew there was something distasteful to my grand-father about these visits. Years later, when McCarthy, by now an Oscar-winning producer, came out with the movie *MacArthur: The Rebel General,* I finally understood why.

The MacArthur family hovered at the edges of my grand-father's life from his earliest military service until his retirement and beyond—witness the Malinta Tunnel—and I think their presence was suffocating to his modest hopes for advancement. Charlie was sandwiched, in age, rank, and aspirations, between two charismatic men of the MacArthur clan. He had scarcely ar-rived in the Philippines during that summer of 1898 when Gen. Arthur MacArthur—father of Douglas—landed there as the commanding officer in charge of the Third Philippine Expedi-tion. *This* General MacArthur, a Medal of Honor Civil War hero and a veteran of the Indian Wars, would soon be directing the Malolos campaign while Charlie was still just a volunteer, and later win acclaim when troops reporting to him mounted a dar-ing secret mission and captured Emilio Aguinaldo. Arthur's son, Douglas, meanwhile, would not graduate from West Point until 1903, by which time Charlie had already fought in three wars; but Douglas quickly joined his father as an aide in the Philip-pines, where the senior MacArthur was by now a major general. Family connections didn't hurt; after the Pacific settled down, the younger MacArthur served briefly as an aide to President Theodore Roosevelt. And after distinguished service in World War I, during which both Charlie and MacArthur were brevet-ted to brigadier general, it was MacArthur who kept the rank of general by becoming the youngest superintendent of West Point in the academy's history, while Charlie—as was usual in peacetime—went back to the rank of major.

To give him his due, though Charlie never rose to the level of Chief of Staff—as did various of his Army War College classmates and also Douglas MacArthur—he wasn't far below it. But while he didn't lack ambition, he didn't have the political killer instinct. And I think it galled him to see the younger man advance, sometimes obstreperously, from the end of World War I to the command of the entire army fifteen years later, while Charlie was still stuck in a peacetime colonelcy. But greatness tells, and while his achievements were tremendous in many respects, while his men loved him and his superiors regularly sought out his opinion, my grandfather somehow narrowly missed stardom. He was not a man of destiny. MacArthur was.

Several times near the end of MacArthur's military service—he'd been relieved of his Pacific command by Truman, causing a national controversy—I remember Charlie and my father, seated at opposite ends of the dinner table, exchanging deprecating remarks about the five-star general. MacArthur, in their view, had been truly insubordinate to his commander-in-chief, and even if Truman was a Democrat, that was simply unthinkable.

Charlie lived in MacArthur's shadow for at least the last decade of his military career, with plenty of time to ponder just how that meteor had shot to greatness. And I think he knew that, unlike his other visitors, Frank McCarthy didn't come to pay homage or recall a shared past. He came to pick Charlie's brain about MacArthur, the military genius and the political nemesis of so many around him.

The red chair, with its narrow waist and erect back, speaks of a strand of family character: Erskine Wood's assertion that

Chief Joseph told Erskine's son to "be brave, and speak the truth." Ohioan James Kilbourne's assertion in a letter that to succeed, he must "establish a reputation . . . with perfect

The red chair

integrity in every trust." Charlie's refusal to promote himself at the expense of his allegiance to duty. In a speech to the young men of the Philippine Constabulary in 1932, he'd said: "Think more of the success of your work, for the sake of your work, than you do for the effect of success or failure on your own record and reputation."

Almost famous.

Chapter 8

LEXINGTON 1960: SOUTHERN CHARM

THE HELL OF AN AUCTION IS, YOU GO INTO IT NOT KNOW-
ing what you will miss most after it's over. And by then, of
course, it will be too late.

A story:

When I was fifteen, I was madly in love with Charles, who
was eighteen, exquisitely handsome, and rarely deigned to notice me.

One day at a church picnic at a recreation area with a lake, I
found myself standing next to him on the cable platform looking thirty feet down at the water. He was waiting for the pulley
to return, to take the hurtling ride down to where you let go
and drop into the water.

In sheer desperation at being trapped in such close
quarters—with, of course, nothing to say—I wondered aloud
what it would be like to dive from there.

"Why don't you try it?" he said. So I plunged off in a dive
three times the height of any I had ever made, straightened too
soon, and landed in the water so flat that I didn't even go under.

"Are you all right?" the minister called, peering down anxiously from the platform.

"Yes," I gasped, knowing, as I lay for a few seconds on the surface, that I was lucky to be in one piece, lucky I didn't land on the lower platform, lucky I didn't go under and start inhaling.

Charles went to the U.S. Naval Academy, became a pilot, and disappeared in Vietnam. I think of him as the years pass and of how sometimes you just plunge without really having any way of calculating the consequences. There was a time when I wondered whether he died suddenly or was taken prisoner. Sometimes I wondered whether he could miraculously come back and all of our lives could somehow pick up where they left off. He and his cohort could be hailed for their bravery instead of reviled, as they were at the time after Vietnam.

We went to a small high school, where everyone knew everyone, for better or worse. But what really bound all of us together in our small Southern town in 1960 was, in a way, the military. Some of us, including Charles and me, were the children of retired military folk. My sister and I were Army "brats"; Charles was a Navy "junior," the son of an admiral. Many if not most of our friends were the children of men who had fought in World War II, most of them officers. One of my friends was the daughter of an airman who hadn't returned.

What drew so many military and ex-military folk, at least in part, to this town of perhaps six thousand in the Appalachian mountains of Virginia was the school my grandfather had presided over—Virginia Military Institute, the "West Point of the South." Here, military families found a certain comfort level, an understanding of what it meant to be military, a reverence for tradition.

Much of the town's history was military. The South's two greatest generals, Lee and Jackson, both made their homes here; both were buried here. Living in Lexington in the first decades after World War II, it was best not to mention Northern antecedents. It was clear you were from, well, somewhere else. Not from Virginia. But Southern politeness would prevail. You could settle here. You were, after all, military, with that code of honor—even though you were technically from that other Army, in a town that still referred to the Civil War as simply "the War." But you weren't really part of the town's internal meditation on loss, history, and survival. Our grown-ups understood that. Once, after I was a grown-up myself, I asked Mother how long it took her to feel at home in Lexington. "Oh, about forty years," she said.

Charlie, my grandfather, was our entrée to this shrine of the Confederacy. He had come as a cadet to Virginia Military Institute in 1891, the son of a Union officer, from a staunch Ohio family. He would return, distinguished after a lifetime of military service, to become the Institute's superintendent throughout another war, the one in which his defenses on Corregidor would withstand siege for five months before falling to the Japanese. And when the press asked him, the much-decorated general, the superintendent, what he thought of war, he said it was a wretched business that he would recommend to no one.

When I asked him what VMI had been like in his cadet days, all he said was that the food was awful. I think he mentioned "gruel"—oatmeal, or perhaps grits? But I have often wondered what life at the Institute must have been like for this somewhat shy young man from the North, whose classmates almost to a man would have been sons of officers from the still recently defeated South, while he was the son of an officer who had fought for the North.

In fact, at least three of our grandparents were the children of Union officers. In later years, my mother would relate how her mother, Bess, had lived all those years in Lexington worrying that someone would look at the portrait of Charlie's father—Charles Kilbourne Sr., West Point graduate and lifelong U.S. Army career officer—that hung in their dining room and realize that his uniform was the *wrong color*. Soon after Charlie died, Mother took it down from its place of honor and quietly stashed it in the attic, replacing it with a nice, valuable lithograph of Fort Monroe, which could be used as a prompt for stories of her and Daddy's younger days in the Army.

Thinking back on it many years later, I suddenly get why Harry Clay Egbert—revered and celebrated in Cincinnati for his derring-do in battle—was never mentioned in the stories around my grandparents' table. He also belonged to that *other* Army, had in fact escaped from Confederate captors three times and gone at one point to Libby Prison.

Of course, we were by now in the middle of the twentieth century, and the town's two colleges were drawing students and professors from the North and farther away, a few even from Europe and the Pacific. But the town's license plates still bore the legend "Shrine of the South." The colleges were all white and all male, everyone went to mostly Protestant churches on Sunday, and life revolved around two poles: academics and Southern hospitality.

And of course there was the argument about who was right and what went wrong, and you could argue it all you wanted. My mother in fact looked through my Virginia history book in whatever year we had the obligatory state history class in school, declared it a pack of lies, and tossed it disdainfully back on my pile of schoolbooks. But the reality was that my sister and I grew up at a time when we all knew people who had actually *known* people who had fought for the Confederacy. Our friends' grandparents were the children of those Confederate soldiers who had marched with Jackson and served under Lee. And as children, we lived inside the town's story, and we took much of it for granted. There was glamour as well as valor in the battles enshrined in statues and gravestones. In a small Southern community, storytelling was entertainment, but also the ritual that formed a common bond. And in defeat, stories become even more important. Victory needs little explanation.

It was not until I was grown and gone from Lexington—educated at a liberal Midwestern college and living many years in the North—that I realized just how much the Civil War, and our tiny town's place in it, dominated our imaginations, growing up. A Victorian horsehair sofa contained your best friend's great-aunt and great-grandmother and from it they arose as the story demanded, everyone knew that, and it went without saying that the furniture was a mute and eloquent player. It bespoke loss and pride, anger and love for a world that was.

Growing up there, with our Northern military family's possessions at last reposing in a final or perhaps quasi-final destination, we'd tour historic sites as children and realize that our grandparents' furniture was much the same as what you might see at Monticello or in Stonewall Jackson's house, right in downtown Lexington. There was the inevitable long sofa of some sort, definitely with horsehair upholstery, which might be designed for comfort or not, depending on whether you intended for guests to linger. The Chippendale was actually comfortable enough to stretch out and sleep on; the Empire settee, however, was stuffed so tight that you had to perch on it. There would be an armchair or two for the gentlemen, and of course ladies' chairs with their lower seats and no arms, to accommodate big skirts with crinolines. And the original crinolines were made of linen interwoven with horsehair—talk about your comfort factor.

Whereas our family furniture dwelt in a modern copy of the "Williamsburg house"—the brick story-and-a-half homes of the American colonies, a Southern version of the Cape Cod—all around us were the more stately mansions and big old farmhouses where the horsehair and carved furnishings resided next to tall windows under high ceilings that had seen Confederate officers and their families come and go. These were typically the houses where the great sitting room or drawing room ran all the way down one side of the house, with the dining room and perhaps a smaller parlor on the other side of the center hall.

It wasn't at all unusual in our childhood for three generations to be living under one roof. The custom was in part simply tradition in an agriculture-based part of the country, and probably grew in the post–Civil War years. It certainly made sense in the postwar years of our childhoods in Lexington, when housing was scarce and women had joined the workforce. You lived with your parents and a grandparent or two who helped mind the kids and keep a roof over everyone's heads. And so to find yourself amid a phalanx of—to us children rather grim—Victorian furniture was not at all unusual, in our own house or somebody else's.

What compels me about all of this, I come to see, is not just my own family. To be raised in this Southern town was to have an appreciation for what was not, always to know the precariousness of the so permanent present. It was to grow up knowing that at any moment a sudden plunge might dismantle your life before your eyes, not to be recovered.

Our furniture traveled for most of its existence oblivious to any chapter of the nation's history that ended in defeat. It knew intermittent theaters of peril, to be sure, and wars from which men did not return. But for the most part it knew expansion, accretion, mastery, and the spoils of victory. In retirement, it finally came to rest in a town the Federal troops had almost razed—burning the military institute but sparing the superintendent's quarters, you remember now, only because Supt. Francis Smith's daughter was just recovering from childbirth, she and her mother and the baby home alone, with the men off leading their troops against the invaders.

And in the same raid, up at the Preston House across town, Mary Junkin Preston, who was Gen. Stonewall Jackson's sister-in-law, hid General Jackson's sword almost in plain sight right under the Yankees' noses—under her *dress!*—and stood right there on the porch with that sword under her big hoop skirt and cool as a cucumber spoke with the Yankee general, and he spared their house too.

Northerners though we might be, we were imbued with the stories: how Lee would have commanded the Union's armies, except that he felt an undying loyalty to the soil where he'd been born; how Jackson was actually from a poorer county to the west, where no one owned slaves and folks disdained government authority in any form, and yet he died fighting for "the cause." Legends of the fall of a way of life, and the enduring myth of gallantry.

For military families like ours, there was this little added irony: The "old" families of this town were all descendants of men who had fought not on foreign soil, but on their own. They had fought against our ancestors in defense of the one thing our professional military family could never really claim: home.

And yes, it would happen one day that a granddaughter or great-niece of General Smith or Colonel Preston would come and sit on the lady's chair or the horsehair sofa in your grandparents' living room, and the two narratives would fuse. Duty, Honor, Country—the mantra of the officers' corps that graduated yearly from West Point to command the Army and travel the world as perpetual military migrants—had come to rest at last, in enemy territory.

❈

SOMETIME IN THE EARLY twenty-first century, my friend Suzanne sends me a double album of songs from the 1960s. The last cut on the fourth side ends with the plaintive, painful cry of the soldier portrayed in Tim Buckley's *Once I Was:* "Sometimes I wonder, just for a while / Will you ever remember me?"

Yes, I say, thinking of our vanished schoolmate Charles and all the others who didn't return from the jungles of Southeast Asia. We do remember you. You would hardly recognize us.

You would find us chastened by this new, this latest war. Our youth and middle years are now a blur bracketed by the war for which we did not forgive you and the war in which we have sought your forgiveness, hanging up signs that say SUPPORT OUR TROOPS. You would be baffled by the yellow ribbons.

I am startled from sleep one morning by a vision of my grandparents, and of their parents, wandering the American

West freely, their passage paid and their futures more or less assured by the American government. Arizona, New Mexico, Wyoming, California. They strode across the Pacific, reaching out for China, connecting mentally with the British raj, in their imagination part of a white man's empire that girdled the globe.

What is hardest to think about is their blithe assumption of the rightness of it all. My grandfather wrote, and much of what he wrote remains. There is a pleasant but relentless flatness to his vision that conjures pre-Columbian Europe and a mindset that insists you could sail off the edge. My grandmother Jeanne writes home from Yellowstone, chatty about the cold weather and the wonderful views and how Frederick Remington's sleigh almost went off a cliff. By the 1890s, Wyoming was already becoming a white man's world, with resort hotels and mittens and sleigh rides. Great-grandfather Harry Egbert takes a bow for nearly dying in Cuba in the charge up San Juan Hill. No one remembers, and he does not seem to discuss, what it felt like to be called to South Dakota in December 1890 in case the Seventh Cavalry might need help putting down an Indian uprising at a place called Wounded Knee.

And Charlie—despite his grim report of the executions of civilians in Peking and his bitter memories of the trenches of World War I—is remembered chiefly for the daring of his exploits in the Philippines and France. The assumption of privilege tends to obscure any other vision of the world.

How do you ever get outside yourself in the moment? In short lightning flashes of dissonance, I suppose. That day on the cable platform forty years ago is as clear as yesterday. I look across my bedroom and take stock of the layers that have made us who we are. One of my father's West Point blankets has surfaced and is folded over the foot of the bed. Its black and gold stripes speak for a moment of the continuity of assumptions: West Point, where I would have gone—instead of the nice safe Midwestern college that proved to be a leftist hotbed—had I not been born female. I'd have graduated a lieutenant and gone to Vietnam and a war where all the rules born in the blood had ceased to be, and there I would almost surely have died, stripped of the immunity that privilege once conferred. Duty, Honor, Country are the stripes of that certainty I escaped by default. By happenstance of gender—and, it seems to me, nothing more—I am alive, and Charles is not.

A cat snores softly on the blanket. The privilege is obsolete, but the furniture—bed and chest and chair and blanket—all these pieces do not speak of that. If I say *We have kept you long enough,* will the life—our lives—drain out of them, or just be reconfigured to new speculations, those of the buyers? At this moment, lying in my grandparents' bed, staring at my father's blanket, all I know is that for some reason that defies rational explanation, generations of people fought, and sometimes died, for things the furniture evoked.

Chapter 9

THE AUCTION

ON THE APPOINTED JANUARY MORNING, WE WOKE, SOME-
what blearily—none of us being morning people—to auction
day: winter sunlight and a light residue of snow on the mountains around us. Jeanne and I had spent the night at a friend's
house in Lexington. She, her son David, and I felt bound to
represent the family in this affair—not that the auctioneers required it; on the contrary, I had the sense they'd just as soon
we didn't put ourselves through the ordeal. But to us, it felt
like our duty to be there. So we choked down some coffee and
headed for Charlottesville, an hour away.

Driving across the Blue Ridge, we talked nervously, justi-
fying each piece we'd be relinquishing, or in some cases whole
clumps. The sandai chest was lodged in my heart. It had sat
next to the Victrola in our grandparents' dining room, where I
would listen, fascinated, to old 78s while the grown-ups went
about their business, their chores, or their cocktails. The front
of the chest with the undulating iron creatures on it was like a
living presence. It spoke of its distant home, which indelibly
inhabited our lives, an alternate reality that was only the thin

veil of a dinnertime story away. My grandfather, sitting at his end of the table, could have reached out and touched the chest as he spoke of China or the Philippines. We slipped casually through the veil with him to those embattled scenes, and to the tropical islands in peacetime, where an officer's pay bought you a lot more than it would in the United States and where servants boiled your drinking water and you shook your shoes in the morning to make sure no scorpions or centipedes were lurking there.

I've been thinking, my sister says quietly as we pass through Charlottesville's outlying horse country. *I feel as if some of these things have blood on them. Perhaps it's time to let go.* We fall silent, reflecting on the spoils of war.

At the auction house, I have my first jolt of seller's remorse as I pause at the big plate-glass windows by the front door. There sits the Federal armchair with what I now realize is our grandmother Big Jeanne's needlework—leaves and flowers in beautiful rich dark reds and greens—and her plump embroidered Victorian side stool next to it. On a table beside them is the tall *famille verte* lamp, originally a Canton vase Bess and Charlie brought back from the Philippines. So here they are, both the grandmothers. Could it have spoken, Jeanne's needlework might have uttered a civil but stiff reproach: *You had no idea who she was, did you? Did you know she played the violin? Did you know how much she loved your father, her only child? Did you have any idea at all what her so very proper marriage might have cost her?* In fact, it will only be months later, as I open one of the objects we did save, a sandalwood keepsake box, that I will discover a cache of letters and clippings and begin to have any notion of who this woman was.

The chair and the side stool with their needlework—the intricate interwined leaves and flowers on the chair, and the little fox, the birds and flowering vines on the stool—they are my first clue. During its life at our house, the chair was covered in

The needlepoint fox

insipid pink linen—by my mother, no doubt, who relegated it to the guest room. The appraiser Sam's ferreting has revealed the chair for something much more than a boring occasional piece.

And the stool—it sat more or less unnoticed in our front hall, overshadowed by the long table with the bowl of jade fruit. Too late now, and what use would these two pieces be anyway, in houses already full, except to take up space and be admired and remind us of her life? I think of the cable platform and of the irrevocable moment after the plunge and before the impact, and I take a deep breath.

By now it's about nine o'clock. We've missed the start of the auction. We find our seats, still in something of a coffee-and-doughnut-fueled daze. The auction house is warm and we're stuck in the middle of a row where we can't get up and move around, or even speak, unobtrusively. Our winter clothes, which were just about right in the early morning on the other side of the mountains, are soon bordering on stifling.

Unless otherwise specified, an auction usually is assumed to be open, with or without a "reserve" price, with the sale going to the highest bidder. There are silent and sealed-bid auctions, Internet and government auctions, liquidation and fire auctions, and auctions variously known as English, Chinese, Dutch, French, Swiss, and Swedish.

Ours is of the type known as an English auction, the style followed by Sotheby's or Christie's. We've decided not to require a reserve on any of the pieces, and we've further described the auction, in its catalog and promotional materials, as an estate sale of the property of Charlie, our grandfather, a.k.a. Gen. Charles E. Kilbourne.

The morning is mostly consumed with china, glass, and the occasional piece of silver. It seems endless. It's wearying. Except for the rose medallion Canton, we're really not all that acquainted with the family tableware passing under the gavel. The Meissen, for instance, is news to us. Meissen? We look at each other furtively: *We had Meissen?* Fifty-two pieces. Must have been Big Jeanne's, because we sure didn't grow up with it. It's too dainty to appeal to either of us, but she did have an eye for the most sought-after furnishings and accoutrements. It goes for $1,100. We exchange quietly amazed glances.

I knew Big Jeanne mostly in her old age, when she was somewhat deaf and accordingly vague about exactly what the current topic of conversation was. By the time I was old enough to remember her, she seemed pleasantly but interminably remote. She dressed well, she seemed to listen attentively enough to the other grown-ups and make appropriate responses. But there was a noncommittal quality to them. They were always appropriate, but somewhat interchangeable, even superficial. I decided that my grandmother was a vain and idle lady, perhaps not terribly intelligent, content to coast along.

The subsequent fate of her furniture in our household only served to reinforce my underestimation of her. She slipped quietly off the earth, leaving her elegant possessions but scarcely a clue about her life—her thoughts, her dreams, her disappointments—except for the sandalwood box of letters, which would lie unexamined for forty years. In our final triage before the auction, we decided to keep the Kilbournes' Chippendale sofa and sell Jeanne's Empire settee, along with her mahogany Sheraton bureau, her lacquered Japanese chest, her dressing table, her highboy, her embroidered stool, and the fine Federal armchair. It was a carelessness I would regret.

Of this grandmother about whom I knew so very little, I have this memory: Right around the corner from the dining room, in the hall, was the straight-backed chair where, when she'd visit us from Washington during our childhood, Big Jeanne would sit, waiting for the rest of us to get in gear for whatever excursion was afoot. There—every minute or so, in one of her more indelibly annoying habits—she would remind my father, who was probably still shaving, that she was ready to go. You could just hear my mother gritting her teeth as she tried to round up us girls and get everyone into their coats while Big Jeanne called out brightly from her perch in the hall, "Well, Maxie dear, *I'm* ready!"

Sitting in the auction house, surrounded by the beautiful, elegant highboy with its fine inlay, the Japanese lacquered chest, and all the rest of the pieces, I am so sorry we didn't take better care of them. The chipped veneer on the mahogany bureau is really inexcusable. I wish we'd seen that needlework on the armchair earlier, but it is way too late to pull it from the auction.

A celadon bowl goes for $195. What *is* a celadon bowl? We have had too little time, in our lives of work and family, to research any of this. We left most of it to the auction house appraiser. But even if we'd had more time, I can't imagine that the celadon bowl would have crossed our minds. It isn't nearly as pretty as the blue-and-white china, some of it Canton, that will later sell for a song. It sat unnoticed for decades in the china closet. We later learn that the cracked porcelain celadon technique was eighteenth-century or earlier, sometimes as early as tenth-century. Oh, well. Who knew?

The twin rose medallion vases go for $375. They are Canton, of course, but have an ugly, stiff-looking Victorian shape, like all that was most dull and proper about the Victorians, superimposed on the magical Chinese porcelain. I can just see a master craftsman in a Kwantung workshop muttering, *Well, if that's what these* fan kwei *want . . .*

When they get to the Canton punch bowl, a minor bidding battle erupts, one that will have unforeseen consequences. Two of our cousins from Mother's side of the family are attending the auction. The auction house has made it clear that immediate family members are barred from bidding. Of course, when the subject came up, we had agreed that it would be unethical for a family to "bid up" its own items. But, I told the auction house owners, our cousins had asked if they could come. Cousins, the owners replied, were not under the same constraint; it would be fine for them to bid and to buy.

The Victorian Canton vases

As it turns out, we will be hugely grateful that our cousins Chad and Elizabeth attended. But as the auction proceeds, their part in it does not go unnoticed. For now, the immediate effect of Chad's first round of bidding is to drive the price of the Canton bowl up considerably. He has a matching set of rose medallion at home that was his great-grandparents', and this bowl will complete it. His great-grandfather was our grandfather Charlie's older brother. They were stationed together in the Philippines, and that—Chad is sure—is where the two vast, virtually matching sets of Canton china were purchased, on what he envisions as a family shopping spree in downtown Manila circa 1903 or '04. Bidding battle won, the bowl goes to Chad.

The morning wears on. The things we care most about haven't even come onstage yet. They surround us, looming handsomely in the high-ceilinged auction house, nicely set off by a number of huge Persian rugs (not ours; part of someone else's share of this auction) and awaiting their cue to enter. There's the bureau Mother imposed on Daddy after Big Jeanne died. It was a better piece than the one he was using, but paradoxically a less historic one, we later realize. Why is it that I'm sure he wasn't consulted about it? Probably because I know that furnishings were basically the women's domain. Men weren't supposed to care what set of drawers their under-drawers were in, and perhaps they didn't. But perhaps I am also subliminally reconstructing that next-to-last triage of the family furniture, when they brought Big Jeanne's belongings from Washington after she died, when Mother did the mental calculus of the "good" and less-than-good pieces, adding to and deleting from the already crowded menagerie at 1 Pendleton Place. That was when she would have banished his larger and plainer former bureau to the basement, replacing it with this Sheraton piece with its handsome spiral columns and rounded feet.

On the auction floor, the Sheraton bureau is, alas, showing its age. Its handsome mahogany veneer is chipped in at least half a dozen places. I feel guilty as I look at its otherwise beautiful face—the elegant simplicity of the inset brass keyholes, the beautiful striations of the wood grain on the drawers. It was in much better condition when I last really looked at it, back in Mother's house as we were packing. The years in un-air-conditioned bins have done their damage. Who'll want it, I wonder. If we had been quicker to let go of it, might it have had a chance of finding a better home?

Like an aristocratic dowager with a storied past, it is haggard now, damaged goods putting on a game face for the world. It goes for $375. Later, on the Web, I find a very similar chest of drawers advertised for just under $5,000. The seller says she acquired her piece at a recent estate sale.

The Hepplewhite bookcase that served for so long as our china closet, the George Washington chair, and the Japanese lacquer cabinet have fared better in storage than the bureau. They are in good condition, and I think as I look around that they represent the three categories of this, our family's final triage. There were the very good but too-fragile pieces, like the chair; despite its value and its good looks, we didn't want to be its curator. Then there were pieces like the bookcase—much-beloved, but put into the auction because we thought they'd do well. We wanted the auction to succeed. And then, like the lacquer cabinet, there were the things we really didn't care that much about.

The stuff we didn't care about was easy. The lacquer cupboard was nice, pretty, but not a piece we'd known well. Likewise the Korean chest with the carved double doors, where I'd kept letters and other treasures. Both pieces were from Big Jeanne's, latecomers to the family mix, easier to let go of. Also among the more easily relinquished were pieces that had been with us all our lives but were either too utterly cumbersome— the ornately carved Victorian vanity with the immense mirror, can't even imagine what it weighed—or simply not to our taste: the unappealing Empire chest of drawers with the curved front and the ashen-colored wood veneer; it always had a spooky and forbidding aspect with its pinched-looking, fussy little brass handles. Or the black chiffonier with the glass knobs, part of a set that we as children dubbed the "nightmare furniture."

In the too-fragile category, with the Washington chair, were the Chinese wedding lamps. Yes, if we were collectors, we'd certainly have kept them, and the huge *famille verte* Canton vase turned lamp. But we aren't, and we frankly didn't want the responsibility of managing these pieces over a lifetime.

The very good but much-loved were the pieces that we'd agonized over, the things we hoped would draw good buyers, bring a good price, find a good home. The beautiful Hepplewhite book cabinet with the glass doors that we'd used as our china closet in the dining room. The sandai chest, with its hammered-iron creatures I'd taken for dragons as a child but which we later learned were Chinese *fu* or *foo* lions, the emblematic guardians of temples, homes, and prized possessions. And the impossibly tall green clay Chinese screen with the tiny figures in black and red—peasants going about their work in fields with oxen, ladies being transported over bridges in sedan chairs, rivers and trees and mountains, a whole mysterious world conveyed in the tiniest, most delicate brush strokes on this huge three-paneled backdrop.

As the auction's midday break approached, the auctioneer worked his way steadily through someone else's china, and the determination of their fate—the unwanted, the fragile, and the much-loved—was nowhere in sight.

During the lunch break, we would later learn from Chad, one of the dealers had seen him making out a check for the Canton bowl. Chad, as it happens, is one of perhaps five men in the family who have carried the name Charles E. Kilbourne over the years, and of course my grandfather—mentioned in the auction's catalog—was another. The dealer had noted the identical names, and after lunch, it seems, word spread quietly but rapidly among the other bidders, who we can only imagine were incensed at the thought that someone who appeared to be from the immediate family was in the bidding.

But at this point in the auction, we haven't yet had that conversation with Chad, and we are utterly mystified. The lunch hour is past, and the auctioneer is well into the big pieces that for so long inhabited our lives. Some of our best things go for so little: the rosewood love seat and the matching lady's parlor chair for about $200 each, though they are in great condition; Jeanne's child's desk, the Eastlake Davenport piece with the delicate carving, for $250; a Chippendale chair, $175; the high-backed Victorian Renaissance Revival chair from the front hall, just $55. The mahogany stool with the needlepoint fox comes and goes, too late to redeem it, for $225.

The huge carved and mirrored Victorian vanity brings $550. As another mahogany chest of drawers goes down for about $300, one of us mutters, *You couldn't even buy the wood in these pieces for that price today.* And now it's the sandai chest's turn. Once more I am looking at its beautifully polished dark reddish brown surfaces, the fierce jaws and talons of the iron creatures on its front, the graceful curves of its wrought-iron handles, and I am conjuring all of its history—the scene inside the walls of the Forbidden City, the blood on the pavement, the dark interiors of the surviving shops and houses, the confines of the courtyard where my grandfather must pass judgment on the supposed lawbreakers who've been brought before him . . . The gavel goes down. Eight hundred dollars. My sister gasps, quietly but audibly. I snap out of my reverie, grasping for the reasons we gave up this treasure. *Just remember,* I mutter under my breath, *not a single drawer of that chest opened easily.* She nods, numbly. *And its iron frieze caught your clothing every time you walked past it.*

The Hepplewhite bookcase

Not for us the shallow drawers, the snagged sweaters. I try to comfort myself with the thought of its size and heft as well. Where would we have put it if we kept it? And yet, the history . . . We are still reeling and well past consolation when the Hepplewhite book cabinet—whose fine blond strip of in-lay, I had discovered just a few days before, ran not just across the front of the shelves, but all the way around them, and whose arched crisscrossing woodwork over the glass front is exquisite—goes for an auction high of $1,600.

By now I'm well into concrete regrets—could we have taken longer, could we have done this better? Perhaps Virginia was absolutely the wrong place for this auction, as kind and capable as we know the auction house to be—the advertising alone must have cost a bomb, and they're getting way less out of all this than we are, to say nothing of the months of work they put into it. Perhaps we shouldn't have billed it as an estate-related sale, maybe that implies distress or infighting among the family? Perhaps we should have gone north, to the region where most of the best, oldest pieces likely originated; it's observable that the only big pieces that sell well on this particular day are Virginian or genuine Colonial in origin—none of them ours, except the Hepplewhite.

It feels as if we have brought the family furniture this far only to fail it in the final hour. We come to the realization too late that it is time to reach out, to catch hold and pull it back. The furniture now joins the ranks of our vanished forebears, carrying with it the memory of those who loved and used it. The diaspora of our fragmented family rolls on.

In the end, the total amount Jeanne and I each net from the sale is less than the cost of one semester's tuition at most liberal arts colleges. But what really astonishes us, steeped as we are in the furniture's ghosts, is the disparity in prices between the different pieces.

The Chinese tapestry, for instance. I'd discovered to my consternation when I looked at the catalog a few days before the auction that its heavily appliquéd and embroidered panels were described as part of a "Japanese kimono." *What?* I'd protested to our auction house appraiser: Charlie and Granny had always said it was a sign advertising the Chinese equivalent of the post office, brought back from that Boxer Rebellion expedition. A Chinese art professor in residence at one of the colleges in Lexington had corrected that impression. It was a turn-of-the-century Chinese sign advertising a bordello, he quietly told my mother, and they had a good laugh. Either way, Jeanne and I had reckoned, it had real value. But in today's incarnation on the actual auction list it's described simply as an "early Japanese fabric." It sells for $200.

Of course, we're not collectors. And these buyers, they can't see the ghosts. We were delighted when the Meissen fetched such a good price. That was early in the auction, and as mentioned, we hardly even knew we *had* Meissen. If they'll drop a grand or so on the china, we were both thinking, who knows what they'll spend on the mahogany?

Who knows, indeed? The rose medallion did well, at a couple of hundred dollars for each half dozen plates or bowls, but the dread Chinese wedding lamps, described as "unusual rose medallion . . . with globular shades with thin walls for the light," go for just $200. ("Those were museum pieces," Jeanne moans quietly. "Mother would be sick about this.") A group of "four cut glass master salts"—which I assure you are quite pretty but also small and not all that useful—are snapped up at $350; but the great clay screen fetches just $250.

This screen I remember from earliest childhood. Like the Canton china, it was already full of its own stories by the time it came to us—of fields tilled and wild game hunted, of draft animals and fishermen and life along China's mighty rivers. For us, the added chapters were of fragility, survival, and the respect owed to an eight-foot-tall, dangerously heavy denizen of the dining room that would certainly shatter if it fell and might also kill you in the process.

Four cut glass master salts

And indeed it did fall one day, but slowly, its chipped edges catching the back of a dining room chair, which broke the screen's fall after my grandfather lurched into it while pushing himself back from the table and arising to go take his afternoon nap. He fell under the screen but emerged, thanks to the intervention of the Sheraton chair, essentially unscathed. As did the screen, with no more than a few more chips and dings along those already scarred edges. In my memory, my mother hovers over him, scolding him the way she might one of us if we had, say, left a wet towel on a good end table. I assume, as I watch her gather him up, that it is because he almost broke the screen.

Screens were ubiquitous in our lives. We used them as walls, backdrops, room dividers. At Army posts in the tropics, woven bamboo screens provided privacy while letting the air pass through and around them. A finely embroidered three-paneled silk screen (*Sold! to the highest bidder, for $100*) lent a certain elegance and dignity to even the most cramped and ordinary quarters. And screens were infinitely portable. I can see my mother and my grandmother arriving at yet another bleak set of Army quarters, resolutely pitching camp. A worn but serviceable Bokhara rug; the obligatory chairs and the sofa, the silk screen behind it; a scattering of small nesting tables that spare precious space by sliding under each other when not needed.

Screens also emerge from one of Mother's favorite childhood novels, which she read to us in turn. Frances Hodgson Burnett's title character in *A Little Princess* is freed from the drudgery of her fate as a scullery maid on the night she comes home to her garret to find the place transformed, with screens, rugs, and fabrics, by a genie in the guise of a kind wealthy neighbor. Screens occupy Matisse's paintings too, as they did the garrets of aspiring artists or of their seamstress models . . . a shred of dignity, something to bathe or dress behind.

At the end of her life, my mother was reduced to a single room in the retirement home. In an effort to make it more homelike, we brought a few favorite chairs—and a screen to divide the sleeping area from the sitting area we'd created. But my mother would not assume the role of Burnett's "little princess," not pretend that a good fairy was going to materialize to rescue her or that bohemian living was her idea of a good time. She banished the screen with quiet fury.

Fragile and supremely unwieldy, despite its amazing survival, the green clay screen was not for us. Much as we might love it, its fate was a no-brainer. An M.D. from the University of Virginia bought it for a bargain-basement price.

≋⚌≋

THE FINAL RUB, THE final wrenching realization in a day full of disappointments and regrets, centers in a paradox. Here, at this auction, the buyers actually have the opportunity to know where these pieces came from. But, I am soon to discover, they are not the least bit interested in any history attaching to the stuff they've just procured.

The auctioneer, doubtless seeing our dismay and perhaps feeling some of his own, mentions sympathetically that families often don't attend the auction for this very reason, because it's just too hard. But for us, like not attending a funeral, it's not an option. We had to see it off to its next incarnation.

We'll discover that we don't really get to do that. As the auction concludes, buyers are already loading their purchases as swiftly as possible; many of them face a drive of several hours with their bulky acquisitions in tow. Only one, a woman from Lynchburg who bought the rosewood love seat, has any interest in learning more. She takes my email address.

Out on the loading dock, the new owner of the clay screen is wrestling it into a van with some help from her mother. *It will look nice with the cream-colored carpeting,* one of them says to the other. I approach them. They brush me off politely. This item is now theirs, and they will create their own history for it, thank you. And who could blame them? Who do I think I am, anyway? I hope they have a big room for it. I imagine a long living room with lots of light. I hope the screen will get to stand at one end, where you can really see it, the dark green and the red and black standing out against the cream background. I hope so.

Meanwhile, after some stiff bidding, the George Washington chair is going to go home with Chad, which makes us a whole lot happier than if it had gone with some oblivious stranger.

As the buyers continue to disperse, the auctioneer almost apologetically adds that the trouble with an item like the sandai chest, for instance, is that they can get the same thing, new, from Pier One or the Bombay Company or some other catalog. *Or think they can,* I retort silently. The chest goes home with a dealer from Richmond. He doesn't even look up as I hesitate near him. By now I'm getting it. Time for us to say good-bye. We head for our cars and the ride back across the mountains.

We stop, again just for the night, in the town where we grew up. We have dinner with friends. They ask discreetly about the auction. They are Southerners by descent, and they understand: We've lost, and we are still in shock. They close around us and the conversation turns to other things.

For my sister and me, the road home—if this Southern town to which our family came when we were children can be called home—still stretches long ahead of us. We are both still living in the North, where we've spent most of our adult lives. We still have jobs, friends, immediate family in these other places, hundreds of miles away. But the only real home our family has ever known is in this town where my grandfather attended the military academy and then returned to lead it, the town where Lee and Jackson are buried. For years, in the middle of something completely unrelated, I've found myself imagining I'm on the town's glazed brick sidewalks, or thinking of the way the light falls on a particular downtown street in the late afternoon. Could we ever really return for good?

And should we have auctioned the furniture in Philadelphia?

Enough. For now we've done the best we could. We've given the memories inherent in the family furniture a decent burial, or at least something resembling a wake. It's over.

Or is it? The parting, the leave-taking, is not so easy, at least for me. For weeks afterward, I find myself waking in the middle of the night, startled out of sleep. In the darkness, the sandai chest and the Chinese tapestry that always hung over it are talking to me. *How could you do this to us?* they say. *He brought us home. You loved us. We were always together. Always. How could you separate us?*

I writhe, toss, and turn over in an attempt to go back to sleep.

Chapter 10

MIA: GHOSTS

S TILL LICKING OUR WOUNDS—WOULD THE FURNITURE
have done better in the North? Should we have kept the sandai
chest? How could we have missed the needlepoint?—my sister
and I went our separate ways, she to her home in upstate New
York, I to southern New Jersey, outside Philadelphia, the
irony of that connection not lost on me.

It was midway through Owen's freshman year in college,
and in the wake of the auction, I found I had some free time on
my hands. As the sandai chest and the Chinese tapestry tor-
mented me with their nighttime visits, I tried to make sense of
what was now history, the latest chapter in the family's and the
furniture's. Would Mother have handled this auction any better? Of all of us, she was the one who could triage with what
seemed like ruthlessness—but, I had to admit, effectively. Like
with that last haul of family furniture, the load she and Daddy
had brought back from Big Jeanne's apartment. She'd taken
what were essentially two whole households of furniture on
that occasion and swiftly decided what would go best with

which other pieces and where they'd all fit in our already fully furnished house. That was when Daddy's bureau was dispatched to the basement, Charlie's father's portrait banished to the attic, and—while she disdained big Jeanne's Empire settee and farmed it out to a neighbor's front hall—room was somehow made in the living room for the lovely rosewood love seat and lady's chair.

If the sandai chest kept me up at nights, the needlepoint was having its say in more subtle ways. It was quietly delivering an indictment of our family's whole set of values. But I didn't get that right away, all in one piece. It came to me after I started to sift through the family papers again, still trying to appreciate who we were and perhaps convince myself that we'd made the right decisions about what—or more to the point, whom—we'd decided to let go of when we auctioned the furniture.

You know the sort of uneasy feeling you get, walking late at night, when you suddenly become convinced someone's following you? Most of the time no one is, of course, and then you feel silly and try to relax but can't because even though you clearly have the street all to yourself, you still feel nervous.

Looking back now, across the more than five years since the auction, I see that in the decisions we made, we were indeed being shadowed, by an unspoken but very well entrenched set of family assumptions.

There was the red chair, for instance: *Charlie, war hero, keep*—versus the pretty rosewood lady's chair: *Big Jeanne, pleasant old lady, suitable seat for guests, sell.* The Chippendale sofa? An appraiser from a museum in Richmond had said it certainly looked a lot like a sofa that had belonged to Thomas Jefferson; but more to the point, it had very likely been in our family for at least five generations, on Mother's side. *Keep.* The

Empire sofa, Big Jeanne's—well, it might have been in the family for a few generations, but look, when it came down from Washington, Mother parked it at the neighbors' across the street; how important could its stories be? And besides, it

Charlie after World War I

wasn't really all that comfortable, you couldn't imagine that anyone in the family ever sprawled on it to read Salinger the way we did on the Chippendale (shoes off, of course, and not in front of guests). So, the Empire settee: *Sell.*

Then there was the Federal armchair with the boring pink linen on its seat. What a perfect example of the hazard of judging by appearances. Hadn't that just cost us our last best chance to spend a little more time with the beautiful needle-work and the woman who'd stitched it? That would be Big Jeanne again, of course.

And I'm struck once more, as I think about it, with the way a family's stories—and, yes, the things that contain and evoke the stories—typically come down through the women in the family. So we were well versed in the history of Mother's side of the family, but with Big Jeanne living in Washington throughout our childhoods and visiting us more or less on sufferance, we knew precious little of Daddy's.

And so we judged—and triaged—the furniture for the sto-ries it contained. The whole process was entirely in keeping with an unspoken family code that I was about to tangle with as I parsed what remained of our family effects. It had to do with keeping up appearances.

Before her marriage, Mother was—surprisingly, given the era—allowed by her parents to live with cousins in Washing-ton and serve as an apprentice at the National Theater. But as unexpected as her parents' relative open-mindedness was, her interest in the theater seems almost fated. I see that suddenly one afternoon as I pore over a picture of her parents, posed in a rare moment together without anyone around them—a news-paper photo probably set up for the express purpose of intro-ducing the new VMI superintendent to his new constituency, the town of Lexington, circa 1936.

What catches my eye is the objects, and I recognize them as a stage set. They are the props and furnishings with which my grandmother—Mother's mother, Bess—created her early to mid-twentieth-century version of special effects. They're the emblem of the social caste to which she and my grandfather,

these two children of the military, aspired—the made aristocracy of the new American empire. They both could claim
lineage back to the Revolution, yet they were essentially pau-
pers serving at the whim of Uncle Sam. *Blow into town, put on
a damn fine show, the men in uniform on horseback; review the
troops—present arms!—the women on the sidelines in silk and
lace and suffocating corsets and stockings and gloves and hats. Silver and crystal, glasses full of deadly artillery punch, an amalgam
of champagne, tea, rum, brandy, and God knows what all else.*
You'd serve your country with whatever passion or sense of
duty you had brought to the task, you'd serve your time—win
a promotion, God willing—and strike the set as sure as any
circus roustabout or stagehand, move on, and do it all again.

Duty. No one was ever just along for the ride in our family.
Your first job was to do your duty, whatever your commanding
officer said it was (in our case, the grown-ups, our parents and
grandparents, since we were, after all, just girls). Your second,
implicit in the first, was to uphold the family honor. And in an
age when dueling pistols were no longer appropriate—though
they might look smashing and make for a great story—
upholding the family honor, for the girls at least, mostly came
down to keeping up appearances.

I see, gazing at the faded newsprint image, how logical, how
perfectly normal, the theater must have seemed to my mother,
raised in constantly shifting Army quarters—there was that
stretch, she recalled, when they moved once a year—as her father rose slowly but steadily in rank. Onstage, the sets might
change, but the parameters were clear, the cues established and
rehearsed. Even when she was giving you her most rapt attention, it was in one of her best roles: that of the audience, which
she taught her daughters well. A stage set, a role to play, lights,

costumes—she'd been doing it all her life and she knew it by heart. In fact she would rarely in her life be offstage.

Sifting through the family papers as I vainly try to lay to rest the ghosts freshly stirred up by the auction, I see that the

The Kilbournes at VMI

family picked its heroes purposefully, and that there were those who didn't make the cut. Its distinguished sons' names reverberate in letters of promotion and commendation, newspaper articles and monuments. Their daughters join the DAR and the Colonial Dames. And so it is an unsettling discovery to learn belatedly of the existence of James Young Egbert. He was Bessie's younger brother and Harry Clay Egbert's only surviving son. We'd lived all of our childhoods with Bessie. We'd heard the legend of how they were left all alone to fend for themselves in the war-torn Philippines, the widow bereft and her three brave daughters.

Now it seems that wasn't exactly the whole story. A hand-scrawled Army memo dated August 8, 1899, attests that James was there too: *Know ye, that James Y. Egbert a Private of Company D of the 22d Regiment of U.S. Infantry who was enlisted on the twelfth day of January one thousand eight hundred and ninety nine to serve three years is hereby Honorably Discharged from the Army of the United States by reason of Surgeon's Certificate of Disability . . .*

But he was nowhere to be found in the family stories, then or later. At the other end of his life, the Army provides the closing bracket too, in a letter from the Veterans Administration to my grandmother's youngest sister, his sister and our great-aunt Kitty: *I trust it will be a comfort to you to know that your brother received the best of medical and professional attention. . . . The place of interment will be given perpetual care by the United States Government.*

I would have been twelve when he died, living with my parents and grandfather. A family death was naturally a topic for discussion and the occasion for a story or two or some fond memories at the dinner table; Lord knows, even though our parents didn't much care for Kitty's husband, for instance, we knew when he died. I am certain James was never even mentioned.

He'd have been in his seventies when he died at a veterans' hospital in Los Angeles. Who was this solitary uncle of my mother, her mother's brother? Was he deranged by his father's death, to be discharged with more than two years left to go, and written out of the family book? For him no words of praise, no offspring to join the DAR. In a letter to Kitty dated 1927—the only other trace of him—he complains about his Army pension.

He is buried in Los Angeles, city of dreamers. And, I begin to see, he is just one of the family members who were essentially, in our lives, MIA. They were absent from the conversation, and their absence there was just the tip of an iceberg. As I sat in my New Jersey living room poring over his oddly laconic honorable discharge, I thought about a photo that had sat, for all of our childhoods, on Daddy's bureau.

In our parents' bedroom were the adorable and excruciating photos of my sister and me at various stages. In the living room were my mother's parents and grandparents in formal dress, and of course that oil portrait of Daddy's important great-grandfather Wood. But on his bureau were his family as he saw them: a soft, darkly romantic picture of my mother in her twenties. His own mother with her foot jauntily poised on the running board of a Model A. A picture of himself at ten or twelve, in knickers with an Airedale. And finally, his father, in a field uniform, holding an infant in what looks like a christening dress.

As a child, I assumed it was Daddy. Until one day, when I was home from college and passing through his den on a quest for tape or scissors, I asked. I was stunned to learn it was his sister. By now, I had been listening to family stories for more than a decade. No one had ever mentioned that he *had* a sister.

Joe Tracy with their baby daughter;
Jeanne and Joe circa 1898 [inset]

I stared at the blond child in tiers of lace and organdy. A sister? Yes, he said. She died when she was two. And that is all.

I don't even remember what I said. Did I tell him I was sorry? For his loss now of some sixty-plus years, for my ignorance, for our collective reticence? For the fact that his family had slid quietly off the familial map while my mother's flourished in story and picture?

Perhaps by then he didn't care. Perhaps he had never minded the skew of our lives. And yet . . . there on his bureau, not one picture of his own children, only a long-ago image of my mother. And his silent colloquy with his childhood.

※|※

IT WAS MY FATHER'S first cousin Marian who finally gave us a few more pieces of the puzzle. It was Marian who had taught him to dance, with their friend Jimmy scraping out a dance tune on his violin in the Tracys' parlor in Washington before some big high school social event. Daddy was keen on some senior named Helen at Holton Arms, the exclusive girls' school that my mother and Cousin Marian attended. Years later, Mother still bristled at the memory of Helen.

And yes, Marian remembered Max's baby sister. Little Jeanne died in South Carolina, our cousin told us, in a mishap involving a nursemaid. They used cocaine then in patent medicines, and like gin or laudanum it was sometimes a quick way of getting a cranky baby to nod off . . . a little booze, a little patent medicine . . . who knew about the lethal effect of an overdose on an infant? Not the nursemaid, obviously. And was it even really her fault?

I try to imagine the effect on the family, a family that never told us the story. Had they gone out for an evening with friends, for one of the post's endless social affairs, for the obligatory cocktails, dinner, bridge, charades? Did they check on the baby when they got home, was the nursemaid someone they knew well? Were they distraught, numb, angry, guilty? How was little Jeanne remembered in the days and the years after her death? Did they leave her there in South Carolina? Did they speak of her at all? No one ever said a word to us about her, except in that one brief conversation I had with Daddy.

After Big Jeanne died in 1963, among the things Mother and Daddy brought back was her jewelry. Still in their original velvet cases lay a number of amethyst-studded pieces that my mother simply put away in a drawer of the black chiffonier. After the auction, as I started to put together the unspoken pieces of family history I'd unearthed, I remembered this: One afternoon in high school, while looking for fabric, I came across the cases in the chiffonier. Inside them, a cross, a bracelet, a circle pin, a pair of earrings, all amethyst and gold, each in its separate box— but what struck me was the cards: calling cards engraved with her husband's name and rank, each inscribed with a message. "To my darling Jeanne from your adoring Joe ... To my darling Jeanne on her birthday ..." It was a side of my formal, placid grandparents I hadn't imagined. I thought of his blunt, somewhat ruddy features and her cool beauty. But it wasn't until later that I heard the story of the elopement.

It was Marian again who told us of Jeanne Wood's less than placid youth. She had run off, our cousin told us, with a suitor when she was barely out of her teens. Her parents somehow retrieved her and had the marriage annulled. Eventually—one supposes after everyone had regained composure—she was courted by and wed to Joseph Powell Tracy, the man who became our grandfather. Marian told us this shortly after Mother's death—again we're haunted by lost opportunity, no way to confirm it—but Jeanne and I were skeptical. Surely something as utterly untoward as an annulment—and then, and only then, her marriage to Joe?—surely even in our diffident family, we'd have heard of this if it were true?

But now, in the wake of the auction, a tiny scrap of newsprint tells me otherwise. It's late one hot summer night, the summer after the auction, on New Jersey's coastal plain. I can't sleep. I'm poking around my living room, looking for something to pass the time, when my eyes finally fall upon the sandalwood keepsake box that belonged to Jeanne. I open it out of boredom as much as curiosity. One more family item to process, this box that lay unexamined all these years, and which I brought back with me finally, when we packed Mother's house. In the end I took it home with me just because it was fairly small—a little bigger than a shoebox—and I was afraid it would get lost in the shuffle.

To my surprise, I find the box is packed to the lid with letters, carefully bundled and tied with string or ribbon. There are a great many letters from my father, spanning his first three decades: from notes in a child's awkward printing and letters from the first journey to camp ("I know you have been awfully busy . . . PLEASE WRITE SOON!") on through high school, when a classmate's doggerel rhymes "Tracy" with "hazy" and "lazy," and into young manhood.

The box is perhaps as revealing for what it does not contain. It does not escape my attention that the very last letter from my father was written right before my parents' wedding. Did Jeanne keep the letters from his married life elsewhere? Or did she not keep them at all? Was he somehow no longer the son she had raised, now that he was a married man?

In the last letter, he writes his mother that he is so pleased that she and his bride-to-be seem to be getting along so famously. "It would be awkward if you took to dueling pistols at dawn or something," he jokes. (Had Mother already given him her opinion of the wedding silver?)

It also holds no correspondence between Jeanne and Joe, as I can't help noticing. This box feels like the heart of my grandmother's life, which she kept entirely to herself, and which somehow survived for decades after her death in my parents' house, apparently unopened and unremarked. It remained, after all the days of propriety and society, after the bracelets and white gloves, after the cake and tea. And it contained the final clues to who she was.

In one of the carefully tied bundles, I come upon a little envelope of clippings. Smaller than notecard size, it is yellowed and completely plain. In it are a short news account of the *Topeka*'s sailing for Havana—"the first warship to enter the harbor since the *Maine* was lost"; four clippings describing my grandmother's wedding; and what appears to be a snippet of a gossip column. The wedding was notable as a double ceremony, in which Jeanne and her sister, Rose, clad in "dainty gowns of white swiss" and tulle veils, wed two young lieutenants, of the artillery and infantry respectively. The brides, one clipping notes, were the granddaughters of "late Medical Director Maxwell Wood, of the Navy, and are society favorites at the capital."

The gossip column—just a scrap, perhaps an inch wide and half an inch deep—tells another story. It contains a reference to a Lt. Hugh Wise, "Ninth Infantry . . . the Army's expert on kite-flying and kite photography," who it avers was "deeply in love with Miss Rose Wood, sister of Miss Jeanne, the whilom Mrs. Bardie Schenck."

I look up "whilom" in Webster's Collegiate Dictionary. "Once," it says. "Former; sometime." *The whilom*—former— *Mrs. Bardie Schenck*. My sister and I had been inclined to dismiss our cousin's story, but here was proof. My grandmother had been married, to the otherwise totally mysterious Mr. Schenck, before that double wedding, which perhaps not coincidentally was a private one. *The whilom* . . . the phrase, casually buried, is freighted with a young woman's public humiliation. Bold enough to run off with someone she obviously cared for, "Miss Jeanne" was brought back by her parents, stripped of her marital status—and, one would suppose, of the notion that her will mattered even slightly in the larger picture of the family's reputation. And she was wed in white, to a presentable candidate, flanked by her sister and sister's groom for good measure.

For a granddaughter of the late William Maxwell Wood, that perfectly proper ceremony—celebrated at an aunt's home and "attended only by a small gathering of relatives and immediate friends"—presumably put an end to any discussion of the matter.

To my darling Jeanne from your devoted Joe . . . Did she reciprocate his feelings? They certainly had a long and successful life together. But as I stare at the little scrap, I imagine my grandmother as a young woman at the turn of the century, perhaps sitting in a bridge foursome shortly after the annulment, her face studiously buried in the counting of her trumps, her ears burning as someone at the table behind her whispers something to a friend. Proprieties would be observed; given the accounts of the wedding, they obviously were. But she saved that clipping—a mere shred—with its glancing reference to her indiscretion, saved it in a box that would outlive her.

It's not until my second time through the box that I find a very small pink envelope. Inside is another envelope, folded over on itself. Labeled "Little Jeanne's Hair," it contains the only memento of an aunt I never knew, the little apparition in christening dress on my father's bureau. Within the inner envelope is a small curl of fine golden hair, tied in a pink bow.

Deeper into the box, I come upon a sheaf of handwritten pages that simply puzzled me the first time around. They appear to be copies of famous poems—one is Oliver Wendell Holmes's "The Chambered Nautilus." The one that catches my attention, in beautiful, careful script, is, I learn later, by James Russell Lowell. Looking at the poem again, I wonder if the copying of it was rudimentary self-therapy:

> *She had been with us scarce a twelvemonth,*
> *And it hardly seemed a day,*
> *When a troop of wandering angels*
> *Stole my little daughter away . . .*
> *And when they had opened her cage-door*
> *My little bird used her wings.*

Suddenly my grandparents' quiet formality seems restraint. Joe's tender messages take on a different cast. Their yearning reverberates in the care with which Jeanne saved those letters from the boy, my father, who was finally their only child.

And my father's private life—was it unexamined? Perhaps. He retired from the Army after serving most of the war as a colonel in the Pentagon, traveling to Europe near the end as an attaché to the generals who were charged with figuring out how to move the troops to the Pacific, in the brief month before Hiroshima rendered that unnecessary.

In the years that followed, he often did not have a conventional job, at least partly because of medical problems. He'd had meningitis as a young man, and its legacy was blood clots that would suddenly appear and start traveling toward his head or heart. The doctors would suggest aspirin and send him to bed. The ulcers he'd gotten while at the Pentagon persisted too. And then there was the drinking. But then, everyone we knew drank, all the grown-ups, that is—they'd been the young madcaps of the Prohibition era, after all—so we didn't think much about that part of it.

He was drawn into managing Red Cross drives or the church treasury, things he did with an easy but not careless grace. He disclaimed any reading more involved than murder mysteries, to which he and my mother were both addicted. But my mother also read Somerset Maugham and G. K. Chesterton and *The New Yorker* and the Bible and anything else her omnivorous mind could wrap itself around. My father sat long into the night in the den, one leg cocked on the other knee, reading a mystery or working a crossword puzzle and drinking quietly but steadily. Hard to know, under the bureau scarves and financial sleight-of-hand that got two girls through college, under the murder mysteries and the bourbon, just who the quiet man was.

A West Point graduate, he was enormously popular with his classmates and excelled when he had a mind to, but managed to graduate in the lowest third of his class. In their young married days, Mother told us of their time at Fort DeRussy in Hawaii, he was efficient and laconic at his desk by day. The handsome, charming drinker came out at night. The Hawaiians, she said, called him *ka punahou*, their nickname for the night-blooming cereus—because, they would joke, that was when he came alive.

On a trip to visit their graves at West Point—again, this was after the auction, ten years after Mother's death—I called in advance and asked an archives librarian if I could see my father's file, from the records the Academy keeps of all its alumni. And there he was, the young cadet. His classmates' limericks describe his affable indifference to academics. He is editor of *The Pointer*, manager of the swim team, treasurer of the debate society. He builds theater sets and parade floats and other stuff—where did he learn that? Years, decades after their graduation, in reports to the alumni magazine, his classmates routinely and wistfully mention that he has not been heard from. *May 1937:* "Max Tracy was ill for several months at Walter Reed . . . but should be back for duty at Fort Sheridan now . . ." *1959:* "No word from Max." I remember, then, a party in Washington one year when I was in high school, how I was astonished to see Lyman Lemnitzer, head of the Joint Chiefs of Staff, in attendance along with about a skillion other generals. My dad was the only one below the rank of brigadier general. He called General Lemnitzer "Lemmy."

Sitting at the table in the West Point library, I slowly become really angry with my father for the first time in my life. I see the wasted opportunity here, of a man who might—*given a little ambition*, I think furiously—have had it all. What Daddy thought about a life in the military, he never said, but I think it can't be coincidence that with all his charm, intelligence, and connections, he never became the general he must have seemed destined to be. He would not be corralled, much to the chagrin of my mother, the general's daughter, who I am sure had seen only the power of his personal charm and not its pitfalls.

Both of our grandfathers, Charlie and Joe, came of a generation that espoused social Darwinism and believed in America's manifest destiny. For all their personal losses, there was an expansiveness and a sense of entitlement about them. For them, looking back, there was remembered glory—or at least the illusion of glory.

For my father's cohort, the rationale of empire was already on shakier ground, its cost too clear, even as they fought and died and bombed during World War II; went on to help carry out the Marshall Plan; quailed at the news from Inchon; debated among themselves Eisenhower's dictum that you couldn't win a land war in Asia; and watched the French go down at Dien Bien Phu.

Daddy died at sixty-seven in a hospital bed after the surgeon had opened him up to have a look at a possible thrombosis somewhere around his liver. But the years and the bourbon had done their damage. The doctors regretted to tell us that he had no liver left.

The letters and documents, and the furniture, are like a weight on one side of the scale. On the other side is life as we knew it with the family. They taught us well—our duty, and how to do it seamlessly. And they left us what they could of their worldly goods. What hangs in the balance is all they did not tell us: of James; of our grandmother Jeanne's first husband, never discussed except behind her back; of her little daughter, who bore her mother's name and whose burial place we do not know. And of her son, the quiet man behind the glass of bourbon.

Max Tracy, circa 1954

What hangs unseen, and inhabits the furniture, is the un-acknowledged cost to them of it all. Yes, they were MIA. They had been for a long time, almost as surely as those who did not return from the battlefield.

Chapter 11

HOME

THEY SAY YOU CAN'T GO HOME AGAIN. MOST FAMOUSLY, Thomas Wolfe said it in his novel of that title, which I'd actually read in high school. Others who've voiced the same thought include Bill Bryson, who went on to remark that you can't best the phone company. Still others have said that it isn't really home we're all looking for but our childhoods; or that home is the place we leave and then spend our whole lives trying to get back to.

Perhaps. In our case, for Jeanne and me, there was certainly no wish to get back to our post-Victorian childhoods. And we had spent our whole adult lives, like good Americans and the military people we were raised to be, moving. Not as often as every year or so, the way Mother and Daddy and their parents and grandparents did. But we knew how to break camp, pack up, and hit the road with the best of them.

The auction had seemed a farewell to the material embodiment of our nomad family's story. The *famille verte* Canton lamp, the sandai chest, the big clay screen—China, the Forbidden City, the dowager empress—gone. The rosewood chair and love seat, the Empire settee, the needlepoint—Big Jeanne's apartment, her life in Washington, the young woman who'd ridden a sleigh in Wyoming and lost her little daughter—gone, living now only in her keepsake box. We'd packed them all up and sent them off to new lives that we hoped would be worthy

The famille verte *lamp that had sat beside the red chair was one of the pieces that would not be returning.*

of them. For better or worse, we'd done all we could, and there was some closure in that.

But in less than a year's time, amazingly, we were packing again—I in my New Jersey rancher, my sister and her husband in their house overlooking New York's Chenango River. We were going back to Lexington.

Henry, my brother-in-law, had inherited some land outside that Southern town where my family—descendants of Union soldiers, for heaven's sake—could never truly be "from-heres," and he and Jeanne had started building there. When I went up to visit one weekend sometime in the year following the auction, there were boxes all over their house. They both still had a couple of years to go before retirement, before any move could be realized, but they were planning ahead—getting rid of stuff and getting ready in stages.

For me there was downsizing at work on one end and a job opportunity on the other. My son was by now finished with his first year of college. I'd fantasized that once he was settled there, I would turn my head toward those mountains where—despite being technically an Army brat—I had been born and raised.

Was it unusual to be so sure of that? "You can't ever have imagined you'd go back!" my neighbors across the street protested over pizza one night after I'd put my rancher on the market. It was now about a year after the auction, and I was clearing out closets, throwing out everything I was brave enough to get rid of, and putting everything else in boxes for a move to Virginia.

Oh, yes, I did, I said to Lee and Debbie. It only took us, what—five or so generations to get an actual house of our own, and I, by God, was going to at least *try* to move back there. I tell them how our Granny—who'd grown up with outhouses or shared bathrooms in any number of Army outposts—had installed not one, not two, but *four* bathrooms in this last home, the only one she'd ever been able to claim as her own. Four baths in their otherwise modest brick house, one exclusively her own and one for her husband. Let the rest of the world fend for itself with the other two, she was not waiting ever again.

So the house was still there . . . where my mother had lived alone all those years after Daddy died . . . and it was mortgage-free and in pretty good shape, and it was ours. All ours. As we'd all migrated around this country, and in Jeanne and Henry's case actually lived abroad for several years, I'd thought often about what a transient culture we are. In my by now thirty-some years as a journalist, it had been my job to report on various aspects of our communal national culture, from North Jersey to San Simeon, California, to Lame Deer, Montana, and a bunch of places in between, and a conviction had grown in me that we were all, somehow, looking for home.

And through no virtue of my own, I actually had—at least I hoped I had—a sort of homeplace, something no one in my family had had for a very long time, something precious few Americans ever have, because fundamentally we all came from somewhere else. Perhaps we're not all first generation, but still . . . still there's that subliminal sense of dislocation, if you stop to think about it, which we typically compound by moving around a lot throughout our lives.

Home? Could I possibly be going home? The whole concept seemed thoroughly arguable, in view of my conversation with my sister out on the back deck in New Jersey that day in the spring. We didn't even know where half the family was buried. The rest are in military cemeteries on both coasts. And hadn't Mother summed it up—her life in the military and by extension ours—when she said it that day with such impatience, or perhaps almost with fury? *We have no home.*

But I was at least going to try. And as I tackled the papers, dishes, books, and general debris of some twenty-five years in New Jersey, I found the old spiritual immortalized by Dvořák playing in my head. *Going home, going home, we are going home . . .*

Whatever we might find at the end of the road this time, we were packing again, hitting the road, still in search of the real American dream: *home.*

As I started to strip the living room to make it more buyer-friendly as per the real estate agent's advice, I looked at those boxes of documents and pictures brought back from Virginia so recently, and the pieces of family furniture and the selected bric-a-brac on shelves and tables—a cloisonné bowl here, a candle-stick there, the sampler and the red chair and its attendant table—and heaved a sigh. It was all going back, where yet more stuff awaited. And soon enough we'd be back there to deal with it all. So if we had known we would move this soon, would we have gone through all the trouble and anguish of the auction?

But the auction wasn't optional. Like Mother and Daddy before us, we were looking at two housefuls of furniture of our own—and all of theirs. As we walked through the auction house that day, it was clear that for all her winnowing, Mother's house had ended up containing well more than a houseful, in-cluding all of those too-delicate, too-valuable pieces we were determined not to keep. There in the high-ceilinged auction house, it struck me that the furniture had never looked better. For the first time that *we* at least could recall, it actually had room to stretch and spread out, letting each piece be seen for all that it really was. Our grandparents' house never looked crowded, but in truth—as we could see, standing there in the auction house—some of these were pieces meant for man-sions; or else each one of them needed to dominate a room, with simpler pieces around it to set it off. It might haunt us still, but the deed was done, and there was a whole bunch of furniture we wouldn't be dealing with when it came time to move.

Still, I couldn't quite get over the fact that it seemed just moments earlier that I had shlepped untold pounds of family papers up from Virginia to Philadelphia, first when we closed the family house, then in the process of preparing for the auction. And of course I got that second batch up to my suburban home only to discover that Philadelphia was actually where we'd *started* from. Now I was packing it all back into plastic bins and preparing to load it onto the biggest U-Haul we could find, come moving day, to truck it all back to Virginia.

❖

CUTTING UP FRUIT for breakfast, I gaze out the window of my New Jersey kitchen. The house sits in a development called Sunnyside, the name of the old farm with its apple orchards that the development replaced. It's a modest neighborhood, from the 1960s, with curving streets designed to slow, stop, or at least befuddle stray passersby.

I think of the apple trees in our yard back in Virginia. It was part of an old orchard too, some of the last of the farmland that so closely encircled our little town when we were growing up. My grandparents were in fact an early part of a relentless wave of exurbia that we are all living through still.

By the time we moved into their house after Bessie's death, the old orchards were paved and built on. The last remaining farmer's cows were still up on the hill above the high school just across the street from us, and you'd hear them lowing morning and evening as they came and went. But in our

Sisters Jeanne, at age four, and Lisa, at age two

neighborhood, the lawns were well established, and the pin oaks, quick to grow, were tall enough to shade the second-story bedrooms in summer.

A few apple trees remained, scattered through backyards up and down the block. We played in them, built a treehouse, bit into the unsprayed Staymans and Grimeses, warm from the sun, and dreaded having to rake them up on Saturdays when our friends were out playing. We joked about my grandfather—in his usual imperious let's-do-it-now military mode—having at the lawn with the electric mower early on a summer morning, without pausing to rake first, and the lawn mower splattering a wake of ground-up rotten apples and the hapless wasps that fed on them.

As soon as he died, Mother had the apple trees torn out and built a fine new brick carport. Of course she was right. It was way better for property values than the old wooden garage on the street side, and more convenient to the kitchen besides. But the carport construction not only leveled the trees; it also paved over my grandfather's cherished rose beds, planted to grace the dinner table and living room with the summer-long bouquets in their deep velvet colors. The backyard went too, with its memories of watering the marigolds and petunias and minding long-deceased baby chicks and pet rabbits. All those were things that required tending. My mother would plant bushes, preferably evergreens, that looked good and required little upkeep.

She set store by appearances—especially first impressions—and was good at them. If you needed a ball gown or costume, she would find or make it, and it would be the best, the most sequined, the most elegant or medieval, as the occasion demanded.

If an appearance was ephemeral, she could and would deliver it in style. The long haul she detested. She would make the long haul if it meant she had done her duty. But underneath the appearances and devotion to duty, she longed to be free.

In the end, she was. She outlived parents and spouse and pets, and her daughters lived far enough away that she sometimes even yearned to see them. And when her life was no longer fun, gracious, beautiful, and under her own control, she stepped off the planet, falling and breaking a hip, then catching pneumonia in the hospital, finally having a stroke.

On the day she died, she was unconscious, but I knew that on some level she could hear me. I sat by her bed in the hospital and told her that if she wanted to get better and get out of the hospital, I would make sure she could go back to the house, and of course the furniture. I had no idea how we would do that, but I knew it had been a mistake taking her out of it. So what if she burned it down or handed it over to some shyster? It was her house, not ours. And it was her life we had unwittingly deprived her of.

She had a living will. The morning of the stroke, the doctor explained the options. Even if she were fifteen, he said, it was doubtful any intervention would help. On the other hand, if we took her off the respirator, she might recover on her own. Unlikely, but he couldn't rule it out.

She died that afternoon. As Jeanne and I sat in silence after the monitor stopped reflecting her heart's journey from Manila to the mountains of Virginia and beyond, I closed my eyes and tried to see her. What I saw was a long corridor filled with a quiet blue. At the end, a small figure turned and waved. I hoped it was Mother.

⋈

IT'S A TEMPERATE July day, and I am driving out of Philadelphia for the last time, at least the last as part of the life I have known there and in South Jersey for the past twenty-five years.

It's my last day of work at the paper. Our New Jersey house is still on the market, but I am bound for the mountains below the Shenandoah Valley, to that mountain village where my thoughts have roamed endlessly ever since I left its brick sidewalks, the old storefronts, the nineteenth-century churches and houses, the surrounding countryside.

Heading from the Art Deco white tower of the newspaper to the Vine Street Expressway, I pass a couple of bike messengers pedaling furiously along a chain-link fence and a few pedestrians on cell phones. The shortest way to our New Jersey home from Philadelphia, the logical way, is Sixth Street straight to the bridge. There's lots of traffic, no trees, and boom, you're there.

Instead, I take Fifth Street North, dipping into the Northern Liberties, then wind back on Fourth Street. Ahead lies St. George's Methodist Church, which dates from the colonial era and played its part in the American Revolution. I drive past St. George's, with its lovely symmetry against the bridge, then across Florist Street under the bridge, past the old Moravian church that takes in the homeless on winter nights. Off to the right is the old original Arch Street Friends Meeting House and a block farther, the Free Quakers Meeting House, which was home to the Friends who broke with the Quaker mainstream to join the colonial forces fighting under General Washington. Betsy Ross was a Free Quaker when Washington legendarily came to ask for her help designing a flag for the new country to fight under. Is it paradoxical that I claim this city only in the leaving of it? As I pass over the Benjamin Franklin Bridge into Camden, I am already focusing on getting the moving van and thinking about who will help us load all the boxes we've been packing for the past month.

At one point during that month, my friend Mary came over to keep me on task. Emptying the clothes closets into wardrobe boxes, I pulled out a gauzy black, white, and gold batik dress, holding it up to see if it would pass muster or was destined for a quick trip to the Goodwill bin. *But it's a lovely dress,* said Mary. *Yes,* I said, *I know.* I hesitated, then tossed it onto the discard pile. *The woman who wore this dress,* I heard myself saying, *doesn't live here anymore. She's about nine years behind me.* But in the end, the fabric was so beautiful, and the memories it conjured so vivid, I couldn't bear to give it up, and I retrieved it from the pile.

Because if you give it up, said Mary as I stood immobilized in the hallway, *there's a loss of self.*

It's the conundrum of the twentieth and twenty-first centuries, objects defining who we are. As life spins faster and faster, we cling to *things* like the flotsam from a shipwreck, hoping that daybreak will bring us to a familiar shoreline. Instead it brings us to yet another venue in which we can or must re-create ourselves, with the option of bringing along selected pieces of the past for comfort and perhaps stability, one less thing to reinvent.

On the other end of the process, there's the letting go. And that's the conundrum redoubled, as our packing, unpacking, and repacking has reminded us all too clearly: Once a thing's invested with whatever an individual or a family has to offer— time and times, power and dreams, memories—who can let go?

Chapter 12

MIRRORS AND SALT

So I CAME HOME—OR AT LEAST TO THE HOUSE WHERE
I'd grown up. A day on the road and a scramble of unpacking
later, the living room in Lexington was full of furniture turned
every which way, including bureaus too heavy to move that
needed to relocate to other rooms, and an equally heavy bed
frame for which the mattress had not yet arrived.

Looking for a way to make any sort of progress through
this thicket of now completely disorganized stuff, I find myself
standing in the shower scrubbing what I'd always thought of
as the Moroccan brass tray with a toothbrush. It doesn't address the real task, but at least this one is finite.

The tray is big; my grandparents used it as a coffee table.
It's been a long time since anyone really cleaned its crevices,
and I think as I scrub that I may be mirroring a chore of my
grandmother's a century ago. Did she always have servants?
And where did she and Charlie get this tray? It's almost cer-

tainly Near or Middle Eastern, and they never were stationed in that part of the world. I know too that they never went much out of their way for furnishings. Among the items we'd definitely have to call spoils of war from Charlie's campaigns in the Pacific and China were the sandai chest from Peking and the Spanish mission chest. Was the tray part of the spoils too?

As I peck at the things I can manage to unpack, the old hall mirror that hung over the Victorian straight-backed chair has just arrived from my sister's house, carefully swathed in bubble wrap, with a bunch of stuff my brother-in-law brought down. In whatever is the reverse of diaspora, the mirror travels home with their first load.

I'd hung another mirror in the hall, a smaller one, older and prettier. But wherever it has been, it doesn't evoke the same ghosts. As soon as I rehang the original, I feel a sense of relief. It captures just the expected amount of reflection, waist level up. It is perfectly, patiently oval, plain and well bred, with a gilt wooden frame and slightly mottled glass. You look into it and it gives you back all of the host-and-guest scenarios that played out in this front hall over the decades of its life here.

Mirrors are eerie things. Like the cameras that so frightened native Americans, who perhaps rightly perceived that their souls were being captured in a little black box, mirrors contain us, and so much more. When we came to pack up the house, we discovered that the elaborate gilt mirror over the fireplace was bolted to the wall. It wasn't going anywhere, and from time to time I would have a split-second waking nightmare in which some reckless tenant threw something in the living room and shattered one of its panels. But we came back to find it serenely intact, and for all of its physical properties of reflection, utterly opaque. Whatever it saw while we were gone remains its secret.

In the room the women come and go / Talking of Michaelangelo. The lazy, almost sing-song cadence of Eliot's "Prufrock" evokes a warm afternoon in polite society anytime from perhaps the 1880s to the 1920s. The women glide behind the surface of these mirrors still, their long white gloves buttoned at the wrist, their hair caught up off their necks, their collars high and their dresses cut very full through the bosom. They are too well bred by far to be showing any décolleté in a parlor. Generations are captive in these glass panels, and it feels as if they, looking out from their ghostly perspective, can see us very well, but to us they are invisible.

Their presences seep out of the looking glass and reinhabit the house, now that we are here and their furniture returned. We are the agents of their renascence. They have been waiting for us.

In its new setting, as we bring the family pieces we saved back from storage, the furniture mingles at first uncomfortably. Like a literal round of musical chairs, none of it can quite seem to find its place. Finally the Chippendale sofa asserts itself, taking back its preeminent spot by the fireplace. I can't tell whether that's a lack of imagination on my part, but it seems it just won't go anywhere else—the inevitability of the living room's feng shui, perhaps.

If there was a place in the house that was my mother's, it was the living room. It seems almost inconceivable now that of all of us in that house, my mother was the only one who did not have a room of her own. My sister and I each had one. My grandfather had his, and it was one of the largest bedrooms in the house. My father had the small den with its own bathroom. My mother had the bedroom she shared with my father, the kitchen she shared with the help, and the spaces we all shared. But not her own.

The living room was the most public space, for while we rarely had guests for dinner, our parents entertained endlessly in the manner of the time and place—a postwar academic and retired military community in a dry town in the rural South, where a casual drink with friends or a full-fledged cocktail party was the norm. The living room was their forum of a weekend afternoon and often well into the evening, as everyone drank a good deal and talked more. Weekdays it sat empty, a room that belonged to everyone and no one.

To situate my mother among the things in the house where she had no room of her own—not even a bureau, for that had been her mother's and before that someone else's—is like coming to Braille as a beginner. I hesitate over the pieces and their meanings, trying to divine her spirit beneath their surface. Pass your hand over the china, the twin beds, the endlessly polished tables, it is not there. She is transitory and elusive as a bird. She hides behind business, always off to type a letter, teach Sunday school, direct a play, pick up food for a party, polish the church silver—and she does it all very well. But if you can catch her unaware, you will find her in the living room, on the sofa, reading.

Of all of us, I think my mother is the most mysterious, and of course that is partly because we didn't listen to her stories as she got older, in much the way we all—including Mother—hadn't listened to Charlie's near the end of his life. I'm reminded of that all too well when I come across the postcards while unpacking, when—in the middle of a box that looks like a straight shot (file this, throw that away)—I run into a handful of postcards from Europe and waste whole minutes sifting through them, trying to figure out whether they're just cards from the sixties that I bought but never got around to sending, or whether these are the cards Mother gathered up on her big trip to Europe with our cousin Marian in the 1980s.

She was so proud of those cards. They were her prompts for the story of that journey, in lieu of photos, since she was totally camera-unready. She told me how she'd given a talk at the nursing home after her return. She wanted to go through them with me and tell me all about it, and I think I couldn't have been less interested. Yes, France, been there, done that. She did manage to tell me about Budapest, how it really was two cities, how foreign and yet welcoming. The rest I more or less dismissed.

To say she is a mystery is but one way of looking at the woman behind the screen of manners, chores, duties, and gestures. Certainly there are many things I know about her, and

Betty,
circa 1954

understand. From her mother she inherited a desperate and steely determination not to fail; from her father, a profligate disregard for personal safety. The siblings she survived left her with a reluctant tenderness for weaker beings, the helpless, those trapped in situations beyond their control.

And through all of her life, there were the books. She stocked our family bookshelves with Somerset Maugham and Rudyard Kipling, Sir Walter Scott and G. K. Chesterton and Saki, Thurber, and Salinger, all of whom she read aloud to us as we were growing up, and we in turn to her. In cleaning out the house I came upon an old, much mended copy of Arthur Conan Doyle's *The White Company*, with an inscription, dated 1920, when she'd have been about twelve: "For Chizai"—her father's pet name for her, mangling a Filipino term of endearment—"for her bravery in the waves off Asbury Park." Like a medal, the object contains emotion, judgment, memory . . . how much less personal than a hug, how much more tangible a token of the moment, wrapped in pages and bindings.

So now, when it is, of course, way too late, and I am left rearranging what's left of her—our, their—furniture, the Chippendale takes its place by the fireplace. Perhaps it is not a bad emblem for her. It is a work of many layers, the last of them the thoroughly unlikely patina of white brocade in which she had it reupholstered after Daddy died.

I see the sofa now as Mommy's talisman, her anchor and her lifeline, in ways we couldn't really have understood, and when we moved her to the retirement home, it stayed behind. It was a survivor in her life. In all the losses and uprootings of her childhood, the sofa was a constant. The sofa and her books, the books and her sofa, where she curled up in the deep unspeaking intimacy that the family shared with its furniture.

Her strengths were also her weaknesses. Her determination not to fail sprang from fear of failing, and she did not fail. But it circumscribed her enormous creativity, since she always stopped at good enough, thereby missing the chance of greatness. She didn't seek greatness; her vision was much more humble and appropriate to a woman of her generation. She carried the ball, as best a woman might, for the brothers who hadn't made it. Always, though she rarely spoke of them, the survivor's guilt walked with her.

The Chippendale sofa

Once, when I was in high school, we were chatting about something entirely different when she turned to tell me emphatically, with no particular connection to anything we'd been talking about, that the most important thing in a relationship is not to make the other person lose face. Another time—we were standing by the chiffonier looking for fabric for some project—she informed me that I was fortunate to have been born female, because, she said, women have more choices than men. They can seek greatness, or they can simply lead their lives. No one will blame them for not trying harder.

Her bits of wisdom came zinging out of nowhere, that place in the house that was uniquely my mother's. Nowhere, everywhere, and the Chippendale sofa.

THE LITTLE THINGS bear witness to how quickly drastic change takes place. In Pompeii's destruction, people are caught in midstep, mouth open, food still on the table. For Mother, our dismantling of the house was her personal disaster. As I unpacked the remnants of the last bin, I was struck again by the fact that the summer slipcovers were still on the sofa, those impervious Dorothy Draper fabrics still almost unfaded after sixty years' use.

She died in the spring. The slipcovers were testament to the haste with which we'd closed the house the previous autumn when we moved her to the retirement home.

Now it was all back, what was left of it—the sofa and other remaining big pieces, along with the books, and boxes of stale-smelling linens that I dutifully laundered for their next destination. The monogrammed towels from the 1940s were still good, in better shape than towels I've owned for just a decade. Maybe it's our modern detergent. Probably we wash them a lot more often. Certainly they aren't as well made.

Box after box disgorged its contents as I made my way through the piles. Then I came to a box marked simply "Kitchen Stuff." I reluctantly ripped off the packing tape, knowing that once again I could probably kiss several hours good-bye as I wrestled with memories and stewardship. I waded through potato mashers, bad 1950s cookbooks with tips on Jell-O in holiday entertaining, cocktail swizzlers, and miscellaneous pieces of worn-out silver plate. I was really glad to find that the meat grinder had survived, and the whetstone, though my nephew tells me it's not really the right kind for sharpening knives.

The dented double boilers nearly did me in, evoking much-hated meals of leftovers. My mother lived by those double boilers, blithely reheating already cooked food until it had lost whatever food value it might have possessed, along with most of its flavor and texture. She was an excellent cook when she chose to be, but I think her early experience of cooking—as a new bride in the married officers' quarters, where she was routinely expected to whip up some supper for whatever stray bachelors had stopped in for cocktails—had left its mark. She'd come to the marriage without having so much as boiled an egg, being herself the child of a ranking officer with a staff of servants. Her revenge in later years, when she once again had household help, was to serve stale leftovers, reheated to a fare-thee-well, on Sundays when the cook had the day off. Unpacking it all now, I found that the double boilers evoked a visceral reaction in me that made me almost dizzy. I had to get a drink and go sit down for a while.

Back at the box, I swiftly sorted the stuff that made me grimace and put it aside for the local secondhand store: the double boilers, the plate silver with all the plate worn off that had become the kitchen silver and imparted the slightly toxic taste of the underlying metal to the food, the spatulas and spoons with the peeling painted wooden handles. As I did, I thought of our dysfunctional dinner table, elegantly set and seething with unspoken resentments between at least two generations of adults. Dinner was really the only time we were all together—my parents, my grandfather, whatever guests might be present, my sister and I—and anything even remotely unpleasant, ill-mannered, or contentious that might have occurred between the adults during the day or previous days would be silently passed over as we made our way through the main course, with finger bowls if there were guests, on to dessert, and then mercifully to our respective rooms. I realize now that those generations where dinner was actually a communal affair were blessed with an aspect of family that's largely lost in a world of kid soccer, karate class, piano lessons, and two-income fami-lies. But while I have some hilarious memories of dinners gone awry, I can't summon a single happy one. The double boilers were just the perfect reminder of it all.

And then I got to the salt. Somewhere near the bottom of the box was the kitchen salt shaker, an unpretentious glass con-tainer with a dented aluminum cap. It had always sat on the stove, its pepper-shaker mate long lost or broken, and held the salt used in cooking. When she was cooking a meal she actu-ally cared about, typically for a party, Mother would taste, then season, then perhaps ask you what you thought of the balance, add a pinch more, and silently nod to herself.

And here it is, grimy from use and storage, still half full of salt, a final and very humble reminder of the heedlessness with which we packed up a lifetime and bundled it off to storage—bundling her off to storage too, that rental unit from which the elderly do not return. I stand with it in my hand, shake it idly to dislodge the salt, then rap it, without success. I show it to my nephew, the rising star among us family cooks. He assesses. *We really don't have a kitchen salt shaker,* he says, *except that wooden one that's always getting clogged up; this one has good wide holes in the lid.* I agree. We set it aside.

Next day I pick it up, move it to the stove, then hastily remove it. It isn't ready for use yet. The salt still refuses to budge, and it's probably as dirty as the shaker itself after a decade of sitting in a dusty carton. I set the shaker in the sink. It'll just have to be rinsed out.

Hours later, I take it back out of the sink and nervously set it on the drainboard next to the detergent. It just doesn't seem right to leave it down there with the dirty dishes. I stare at the shaker, my hands defensively on my hips. What *is* it?

It's that this salt, inside this shaker, was last used by a woman now more than ten years dead. For a quarter of a century or more, she knew this salt shaker just as I see it now, and the salt that I am about to rinse down the drain was put there by her. She was the last person who touched the shaker—not counting whoever threw it in the carton for storage. It must actually have her fingerprints on it. She shook it over some meal that she cooked to share with the dwindling but undaunted circle of friends, the elderly widows who maintained gaiety and a stiff upper lip for the world to see; or perhaps a meal she cooked for one of us, when we deigned to visit, which wasn't as often as she'd have liked.

When we did show up, she greeted us at the door with a little shriek of delight, stocked the refrigerator for us, and cooked the meals she knew we'd like. And in return, when she showed signs of frailty, we descended on her world like scorching lava and swept it all away—the candlelight dinners, the novels by the fire, the cocktail parties, and the place that held the memories of countless years of roses and damask, drinks on the warm stone of the terrace, friends who dropped in from town or journeyed from the ends of the earth bringing their tales from some outpost of the American empire, that world in which she was the general's daughter and the colonel's wife.

She'd kept the place almost as her mother before her had left it. And then on a warm October day it vanished into boxes, not to return in her lifetime. This wasn't, of course, anything remotely like the cataclysms humanity routinely inflicts upon itself. Not even like the disasters that drove her ancestors, among so many others, to these shores. It is a small epic, a microcosm. But for her, it was the end of the world she knew.

I find myself thinking of how, in generations much more remote than those who sat at our dinner table, the nearest of kin would get down into the open grave and take their loved ones in their arms, wrapped in a winding sheet—no coffin wall between them—and literally lay them to rest. They embraced life, precious and unpredictable, even at the last possible moment, and they faced up to the reality of death. By comparison, our so willing embrace of the impersonal care facility seems weak and heartless, our ceding of the death rites to a funeral home a desertion of those we love.

I stand staring at the salt petrified in its slender glass container. It touched her hands. She ate of it. It is a last, very concrete and yet so ephemeral thread connecting me to the woman who brought me into this world I now inhabit. Like magic, it will disappear if I wet it. The container will be clean and ready for new use.

It feels wicked even to think of pouring my mother down the drain. Too late, though. That moment, the opportunity to have those unspoken dinner-table conversations, fled ten years ago and counting. I leave the salt shaker, with all its accumulated grime, and put everything else in the dishwasher.

A friend calls late in the evening, and is surprised to find me distraught. I know it is ridiculous after all these years, I tell him, but I am grieving.

⁂

IT WAS TEN YEARS after Mother died, and after the auction, that our cousin Gordon fell and broke her hip. She was living outside Baltimore, where she'd spent most of her life. Gordon was the youngest of Mother's first cousins, one of five siblings who were essentially our solitary Mommy's brothers and sisters growing up.

Gordon went to the hospital, was sent home, got worse, and was sent back. She kept telling them her hip hurt, but, frail as she was, her stoicism evidently gave her the appearance of being on the mend from the fall, and it seems it didn't occur to the staff to probe. As we took turns sitting with her in the convalescent home, she talked more about how annoyed she was with herself than she did about the pain.

But eventually the pain won out. And now she was dying.

I got to Baltimore just as they were moving Gordon from the ICU to a small private room in the med/surg unit—where, as her niece Virginia remarked, they move people when there is nothing more they can do. Now she was mostly sleeping, and when awake, not very coherent. I thought of our last couple of days with Mother: the fear and worry in her eyes, the inability to talk, the thirst.

And I thought of the afternoon when we took Mother off the support systems and let her die. Like Gordon, she had a living will. Was it what she wanted? Is it ever what anyone wants? And even if, when they wrote out the will, they knew it was the right thing to do, does it still feel that way in the moment when they are standing on the brink, swaying, poised to plunge off into we know not what? In their wills, they said they wanted no extraordinary means. But when they were at last lying there, beyond words, too weak to move, didn't they want to live another day, another hour, another year? Did they not fear the abyss? The whole process remains unfathomable if you are standing outside it.

In her new room, Gordon, in a fresh hospital gown and on dry sheets, breathes peacefully, almost snoring. When the nurses had turned her to change the bed, she clung to us like a drowning person. All that strength was concentrated in her arms, her little clawed hands, drawn up now in sleep on her chest. Her eyes, when she opened them to look wildly around, were frightened but cognizant: *Where am I?*

She has beautiful bones, a better nose than my mother's, but the same weak chin. She has her mother Adelaide's once-dark hair, now white; dark eyes, strong brow—forbidding in the older generation, here tempered with gentleness, mirth, and the unqualified assurance of having been well loved by at least one other person, the husband whose letters from World War II are neatly packed in boxes at the apartment she won't see again.

The room is quiet and dry and light. It looks out into a bank of pine and oak trees, where a breeze is playing. It's a beautiful day, as several nurses have remarked—especially if you are looking through plate glass and don't have to contend with the 90-degree humidity outside. All in all, if you were old and very tired, it would not be a bad day to let go.

On the wall is a pastel of a mountain meadow with a winding, fast-running stream. It makes me think of canoeing the rapids on the Delaware, and then of the hard truth that no matter how beautiful a day it is outside, Gordon will not feel the warmth of the sun on her shoulders or the breeze that moves the trees outside her window. She won't taste fresh air again. I'll leave and go home, and when evening comes I will be breathing the cool nighttime air that comes up off the grass, and she will not.

❦

GORDON DIED WITHIN DAYS, before I could get back from Philadelphia for another visit.

Her death touched me in a way I frankly hadn't allowed Mother's to do. Mother was our *mother,* and the thought that honoring her living will might actually be a betrayal was just too awful even to contemplate. So we fell back on the family stoicism. The minister and his assistant actually marveled at how calmly we picked out the hymns for her memorial service. We knew just what she'd want, and we got right on with it.

But Gordon wasn't Mother. I could sit by Gordon's bedside and see her in a way I couldn't see Mother. And as I drew closer, at her bedside, I could see all of them in her drawn face. I saw Gordon as the young woman who'd been my mother's cousin, and their mothers who had been sisters together in the Philippines, and the bright young men they had married, and all they had done and been, and tried to do and be.

Gordon, youngest of them all, had been fussed over and allowed a gaiety that perhaps the others didn't get to show, or claim. She'd shared that gaiety with us, laughing at life and encouraging us to laugh too. And the remembrance of her gaiety when we were young, and her courage in her loneliness at the end, opened a seam, just a little tiny crack perhaps, in my unfinished grief.

That afternoon by Gordon's bedside continued to haunt me, and it led me back to Mother's. We had done what Mother said, the afternoon she died, but had we done our best? For once, there were none of those unspoken but tacitly understood rules. We were flying blind, and it was anyone's guess whether an eighty-three-year-old woman on the edge of death—say, ourselves, several decades from now—might not clutch fiercely at a reprieve, however tenuous, if it were offered.

Gordon's death opened the door, just that crack, to the mourning process. And then, like a cascade, came the move, the retrieval of the remains of the family furniture from the bins, the mirrors, and the salt.

And it occurred to me, finally, to wonder: Just when was it exactly that our Mommy—who maybe was pretty nervous about even having children, let alone having the responsibility of bringing them up, but who saw to it that we were clean and fed and got read to and had a new dress to wear to school in the fall, and later, a dress to wear to the dance—when was it exactly, sometime in our adulthood, that she became that more formal "Mother"? Sole survivor among her siblings, perhaps afraid for her own survival, certainly afraid for her children's, since up till then every important child around her—that is, her siblings—had died, and for all she knew, in her child's mind, it might have been her fault that they had. And who could never be the son of a military family, merely someone's daughter or wife, who had no sons of her own.

She was the child, grandchild, and descendant of those generations who ingrained in her and in us their awful, useful, implacable stoicism. All of them in the furniture, in the mirrors, in the house, with all the stories told and untold, never to be heard again. The stories were of survival, even heroism, in battle, of victory on the battlefield and in the drawing room. They were gripping, clever, sometimes amusing. But they did not speak of children lost to fever, or of young men who in some way had failed to measure up. Those who survived came back to tell their tales, but they'd left pieces of their hearts strewn from the shores of the far Pacific to the graveyards of the East Coast.

And to the roll of those missing in action, though she hid it well, I could add one more: our clever, efficient, stoical, and dutiful Mommy.

My mother's salt shaker

Chapter 13

THE GATHERING

WE'D SEEN THE AUCTION AS OUR CHANCE FOR CLOSURE, a farewell to more than just the furniture. It was an act of faith, but also something akin to scratching a mosquito bite—a reflexive impulse that is logical enough on the surface of it, but does not solve the underlying problem. The furniture we'd sold was gone, for sure; but its companion pieces, and all of their collective stories, were still with us.

But if this was our problem, it also contained the seed of our salvation. So I think it was not coincidental that as I sought to lay to rest whatever ghosts I could and let go of the things they inhabited, I also took to the road.

From the now-reunited family papers, which the women of the family had saved and passed on for generations, I began a journey. In the journey was a kind of healing, the healing that resides in stories.

By journey's end, its stages had taken me from the East Coast to the West and had included a ship's reunion, a side trip en route to a national park, and a flight across the Pacific. They spanned less than four years in all. They were unconnected by any conscious motive at first, but as I traveled a purpose emerged, and gathered force. I was gathering family.

CARLISLE, PENNSYLVANIA, 2004

Driving through Pennsylvania on part of the quest for family, I passed through a series of lovely old towns, and I found myself passing through time again. Their houses front directly on the street without the intermediacy of lawns or shrubs; no screens here. Their commercial districts struggle for relevancy in a world of strip malls and computer shopping; their once-proud town squares emanate a forlorn dignity. This, I thought, is America—the one we talk about when a crisis like September 11 strikes. This is the America we fight for . . . and fight from. These are the towns from which the young men and women march, from which mills once fed and clothed the world or in which their products were sold to the thousands of middle-class families. From Maine to Pennsylvania, down the East Coast, west to Ohio and beyond, the brick and frame buildings are as charming as ever, but how many of us care to live in such close quarters these days? Not, certainly, the homeowners and builders who have gobbled up the farmland surrounding the towns and put up cookie-cutter homes of faux stucco and wannabe clapboard. No, these houses are narrow and small, and so are their backyards. The traffic crawls past them. There is little privacy. This is the America we imagine we are protecting, the one on which we have drawn in every war. And it is looking a little shabby now, and deserted.

My grandfathers would have recognized these places. One such town is Worthington, Ohio, settled by Kilbournes in 1802, hacked out of the wilderness with scarcely a nod to those other Americans who preceded us. Another is Towanda, Pennsylvania, where Tracys and Powells lie buried on the hill overlooking the town and the river that powered its mills.

I am left thinking, as I drive on through the remnants of Pennsylvania's farmland east of Harrisburg, of the America my grandfathers believed in. By the time they so proudly set off to defend it, the ideal was fast becoming a commodity to be exploited by the Gilded Age's men of means. Yet the country had recently fought itself to a standstill at least partly—in the eyes of idealists—over the right to be free. And reaching back further, to the ministers and ship's carpenters and Quakers and soldiers of the century before, we see that there was always that idealism, and a very eighteenth-century belief in the rights of man.

I return across the haunting farmlands and through the haunted villages and wonder where we are going. Wonder what my grandparents, footsoldiers of the American empire, would think if they could see us now. Wonder if they would even question what had become of their vision and their dreams, or whether all of this would simply seem like progress, the very logical extension of all that they set in motion.

And if they could have seen all that their generation was setting in motion, would they have lived their lives any differently?

CHICAGO 2004

I meet Owen and some cousins from Daddy's side of the family in Chicago, where a ship's reunion is in progress for the crew of the U.S.S. *William M. Wood*—named for that great-great-grandpa, the first Navy surgeon general.

It's seven A.M. on our second day here, and we are on a bus full of aging veterans who served on the destroyer at some time between 1945, when the ship was commissioned, and the midseventies, when she was decommissioned, eventually to be sunk in target practice off Puerto Rico. For most of its life, the U.S.S. *Wood* steamed peacefully back and forth across the North Atlantic, with stays in Newport, Rhode Island, and in the Mediterranean, and a couple of Cold War missions that entailed some risk. The guys on the bus span most of the ship's lifetime. We are all wearing navy blue baseball caps with a logo of the ship stitched in gray thread over the bill.

It's November, and it's cold and dark, and that makes it seem all the more ungodly early in the morning. As you may recall, we are not morning people. But we are bound for a tour of a naval station on Lake Michigan that's the Navy's principal training post. It's the station where many of the vets on this bus trained, and since Owen is of military age and we are in the middle of a couple of wars, as it seems, I want to see it with him. Does he need to be part of all that? If he does—this son of ours who has mentioned to me once or twice that the military is offering cash bonuses that could help finance his education—I think he should look at some of what it might entail. Like this training post.

At the naval base, we attend a spectacular graduation "pass in review" ceremony (a class of five hundred or more is graduating every Friday at this point in the base's history). Several young sailors actually faint—from the stress, I guess—during the drill in the vast graduation hall. We tour the campus with its hundreds of buildings—more than 10 million square feet of occupied space—the first of which were dedicated by President Taft in 1911. We drive along the waterfront and eat lunch at the officers' club. I know for the men, the vets, there must be so many memories of their youth, spent upholding those ideals we learned in junior civics. For Owen and me, there's the opportunity to try to peer discreetly through the barracks windows into the lives of the current generation. The afternoon concludes with a memorial service in remembrance of more than two hundred veterans from the U.S.S. *Wood* who are no longer alive, and the Navy hymn: *O hear us when we cry to thee / For those in peril on the sea.*

Later, back in Virginia, a friend tells me he thinks our schoolmate Charles has perhaps been accounted for—Charles, who also served in the Navy, but did not survive the peril of the air. I go to the Department of Defense website. In 1991, Congress passed a bill offered by ex-POW Senator John McCain directing the department to make information publicly available, subject to families' consent, regarding soldiers still classified as missing in action from Korea, the Cold War era, and the Vietnam War.

A Library of Congress link leads to the Vietnam era POW/MIA database. The site is searchable by name, the information for each entry coded, with terse translations of the code in a separate section of the site: *date, 68; rank, 03; country, NV; aircraft type, F4J.* Charles was a lieutenant commander, flying a fighter jet over North Vietnam, when he was lost in 1968.

The code for "status" is bleakly inconclusive: *XX. Presumed dead.* He was twenty-five, one of thousands who died there, just about the same age as my grandfather when he went to the Philippines. A second website contains his radar intercept officer's account. Their plane was hit on a bombing mission and burst into flames. The intercept officer ejected safely, only to be captured and taken to Hanoi. He did eventually win release and return to a country that reviled his war, to report that he believed his comrade and commander had gone down in the burning plane.

Fort Verde, located in a state park near the town of Camp Verde, Arizona, isn't that block fort you see in the movies. It's a bunch of disconcertingly ordinary-looking bungalows, kind of like Cape Cods but in adobe, with wide roofed porches against the Arizona sun and little vegetable gardens out back. A guide told us that during the late 1870s and early 1880s— when Bess's family lived there—the closest the Indians typically came was to the foot of that bluff across the arroyo. By then Geronimo was gone, eventually to be captured and imprisoned in Florida, then Alabama, and finally Oklahoma, where he'd die of pneumonia and probably a broken heart. Only a few stragglers were left of his people around Fort Verde, perhaps wondering if they'd get shot if they asked for a little work or some food.

The house my grandmother actually lived in as the five-year-old daughter of a commanding officer has been restored. I stood in disbelief at the top of the stairs, looking through the plate-glass humidity barrier. In summer, when it was so hot, everyone slept downstairs. But in winter, this might actually have been her room, with a single bed, a quilt, a window from which she could look out toward the arroyo. Perhaps a copper tub like this one was actually here. Perhaps a chair or two. Did she have a doll? Did they really have a pump organ, did someone from earlier leave it, did she learn to play? Was she afraid of the Indians? And did she like Lieutenant West and his wife? Did her two brothers sleep across the hall, and were they pests? Was this where her older brother Francis died of some childhood illness?

When she slept in this house, this bleached Army bungalow, she was the same age I was in the year she died. She was here, really here, *in* this room. There is a visceral feeling, almost like a

At Fort Verde: the bedroom where little Bess might have slept

sigh of relief, in reclaiming my grandmother's childhood, even for a moment.

WOUNDED KNEE, SOUTH DAKOTA 2006

This was arguably a less creditable part of the family's history, though of course they didn't think so. They thought they were right. They were God-fearing Christians, bearing the "white man's burden," come to rescue the native population from sin and savagery in the euphemistically titled Indian Wars.

With a friend, I drive to Wounded Knee, in the southwest quarter of South Dakota. There the U.S. Seventh Cavalry in late December 1890 slaughtered three hundred Lakota Sioux, many of them women and children, who were traveling with their dying leader Big Foot through the deep snowdrifts and winding trails and passes of the wintry Badlands to seek refuge with the Pine Ridge Sioux. There at the Pine Ridge agency, they had agreed, they would surrender. But they were intercepted, and the massacre became the last official battle in the painful history of the Indian Wars.

Harry Clay Egbert's military record for December 1890 through January 1891 is curiously laconic. He had been stationed in Wyoming when he was suddenly transferred for six weeks to South Dakota. That's all it says. So I called the Army War College in Carlisle, Pennsylvania, and spoke with a reference librarian. *Oh, yes,* he said. *The entire country was in a panic about this supposed Indian uprising. They sent Army detachments from all over to Wounded Knee, to back up the cavalry.*

These days, a barren, windswept cemetery on a hilltop bears witness to the work of the Seventh Cavalry. I left an offering of tobacco, tied with a red thread, at the foot of the Lakotas' monument that bears their names, and said a prayer. Then we drove back into the twenty-first century of the Pine Ridge Reservation, and a few miles up the road on another hilltop, we stopped to eat at Betty's Kitchen, a small but very busy restaurant in the kitchen of a modern rancher. A busload of tourists was disembarking to pick up box lunches while the local politicians talked at a table over buffalo burgers and

Betty's grandkids played in the living room on the other side of the divider from the rancher's kitchen. We ate, and started the long trek back to the interstate.

It was April when a friend persuaded me that I really ought to go with her on a tour of the Philippine Islands. She wanted company, and besides, hadn't my family lived there? This trip, she said, would do me good.

And so I went, hoping of course to find the family stories leaping out at me from every corner. Manila, where Charlie shinnied up the telegraph pole in the middle of a burning neighborhood near the Paco Bridge. Manila, where Carlos and Mother were born. Manila, likely source of the mission chest, former home of the sandai chest, those cues for so many of their conversations over the dinner table.

In Manila, I thought Charlie might be remembered. When I found that our guides had never heard of him, I was a little disappointed, but then, on reflection, not surprised. After all, the tunnel that was perhaps his greatest achievement was built under cover, with the pretext of improving Corregidor Island's transportation, so at the time there would have been no official record of its real purpose. And after the islands' liberation, the war was fast ending and a new chapter of Philippine history beginning, a chapter notably freer of American influence and any need to look back at it.

A two-hour ferry trip to the island of Corregidor in Manila Bay attests to the remoteness of the island in the days of Charlie and Douglas MacArthur. Originally, it was the place where ships stopped for inspection, where their manifests and cargo were determined to be legal—"the place of correction." Near the ferry landing, we found the old concrete pier from the 1930s, from which the rail tracks still lead up Malinta Hill toward the tunnel—the tunnel where, despite its ostensibly peaceful purpose, tons of emergency supplies and armaments would be deposited.

You can tour the main tunnel. It's less than nine hundred feet long, and it remains essentially as it was when they dug it,

The Malinta Tunnel

give or take the fallout from five months of incessant shelling during World War II and the slow attrition of the years since. Its battered beams and rock walls are a stark contrast to the lush foliage that has since covered the island with greenery and bright blossoms and fruits. A "light and sound" show plunges you into darkness as the tunnel vibrates with the sound of shelling, then illuminates one of the side tunnels, where eerie bronze figures evoke the underground hospital and the communication center with soldiers in headphones.

MacArthur stands in bronze at the seaside loading dock, as well as in the tunnel, where he's giving orders as the bombardment continues. As we emerged into daylight, our guide— apprised of my mission—asked how I felt. *Amazed,* I told him, to think that I was standing right now on a spot where my grandfather had almost certainly stood when he was just about my age, while the tunnel was under construction—ten years before it would be used exactly as he intended, in a war he had foreseen but would not be part of. Instead, his old friend and nemesis would find shelter and a well-equipped fortress in the Malinta Tunnel.

Now we were walking the parapets of the gun batteries he'd built in 1909, peering into their underground bunkers and ammunition storerooms. SILENCE, said a sign posted by one of them. "Spooky" was the verdict of a young man who was emerging as we went in.

For me, the spooky thing was not the decaying fortifications, or the guns now almost a hundred years old that my grandfather might have touched the day he first ordered them fired in 1909. The spooky thing was to find him waiting for me at the Hotel Corregidor, where we ate lunch.

I'd wandered into the gift shop, hoping to find some little presents I could take back to the family. It was all generic cups and refrigerator magnets and ashtrays with cutesy slogans like "I Brake for Geckos" or "I ♥ Corregidor." Frustrated, I paused en route to the cash register at a rack of buttons. I hate buttons. I never buy them. But I idly spun the carousel they were pinned to, and as the back side came around, I saw one—just one—that had a vaguely familiar face above what looked

The button

like a West Point uniform. *Huh,* I thought, *must be MacArthur.* I'd buy it, despite our family's opinion of the man. MacArthur as a West Point cadet, well, at least it was something. Such a young face, so open and unmindful of all that lay ahead. I took the button off the rack and looked closer. *"Lieutenant Charles E. Kilbourne."* The picture was of him in his VMI uniform, his senior picture for the 1894 yearbook at the military institute in Lexington. The inscription around the button identified him as the first garrison officer of the island, circa 1908. In the photo, he looks about twelve years old.

What were the odds? Why a button of him at all, and one that showed him in his youth? It must have been left over from some centennial celebration of the Philippine-American War and his pole-climbing exploit. Who knows? It was enough. I tucked it into my bag, and spent the rest of the day almost giddy with elation. I hadn't come in vain. They *had* been here, really here, and it had mattered to someone.

Late that afternoon, the Corregidor tour made its final stop for the day at the big Pacific War Memorial, which commemorates all who fought and lost their lives in the Pacific theater. There, in a little museum behind the ruins of the Corregidor post's cinema, I found him again. A wall exhibit of the island's history before World War II included two letters of recommendation for a Filipino family named Medina who had lived on the island for more than a century before the war laid waste their fishing village. At the bottom of each letter was the familiar signature, clearer and less shaky than I remembered it from when I was in high school, near the end of Charlie's life.

I was immediately transported back to his room at home, which smelled of pipe tobacco and pencil shavings. I was bound for a big dance at VMI. His VMI. Mother coaxed me to go show him how nice I looked in my white gown, a tradition for girls at the Ring Figure Ball. "Go on," she nudged. "He'll be so pleased."

"Very nice," he said in a lukewarm tone of voice, peering up from his reading. "But you're wearing too much lipstick."

Right. *Too much lipstick*. Ever the commanding officer.

When he came to the Philippines, he was a young man. He did his best according to what he'd been raised to believe. His tunnel saved lives, both American and Filipino, in the desperate days near the end of the war in the savagely contested Pacific theater. Perhaps it even, in its way, helped change the course of history, leaving the Philippine Islands in the hands of Americans who'd pledged to release control of the territory, and did.

Again, that visceral feeling: *Here they are. This is who they were, and they are part of us.* I mourned them all, even in their human fallibility, from which we haven't yet by any means weaned ourselves. I mourned the people they pushed aside, and all the struggles and misunderstandings, tragedies and arrogance on which a country is founded. And I began finally to lay this family to rest—scattered, like so many Americans', though their lives and graves might be.

EPILOGUE

Back in Virginia, just before Christmas after my return from the Philippines, three generations of the family were coming and going and sometimes staying at 1 Pendleton Place, as Jeanne and Henry finished building their house and their grandson, Gabriel, settled into third grade at the school down the hill. But this time—again, in a moment's time, just a little more than half a century—my sister and I were suddenly in the oldest generation. In an eyeblink, it seemed. Five generations by now had lived here, from the oldest, Charlie and Bessie, to the youngest, Gabriel—five generations, and, nomads that we were, we still weren't settled.

At one point, with everyone going in different directions and the house in chaos, I engaged a service run by two local women to help me clean, and April and Kay came every few weeks for several months. One morning in the late winter or early spring of that year, I happened into the kitchen as the two of them were moving into high gear. I'd asked them to really, really scour it. What with all of us coming and going, it was all I could do to keep up with the meals, the dishes, and some laundry. I came in as they were washing baseboards and windows, scrubbing appliances, wiping down cabinets, and cleaning the clutter of small objects.

Kay's at the back door, washing its windowpanes. April's working on the stove. The first thing that catches my eye is the salt shaker, which has by now resided, half-empty, for several years on the windowsill above the sink.

My mother's salt. The shaker is sitting *in* the sink, full of water that is slowly dissolving the crystals. Soon it will be no problem to just dump it all right out, and voilà! A clean—and even functional, if somewhat battered—kitchen implement. And, without its salt and accumulated kitchen grime, completely anonymous. It could be in a flea market, yard sale, or thrift store, and you would never even notice it.

"Oh, *no!*" I gasp as I stand at the sink.

"What?" says April, looking up from the stove.

"Oh," I stammer, "you . . . washed the . . . salt shaker."

"Well, *yeah*," says April.

I say, "It's just that this was my mother's"—I am at that moment realizing how ridiculous it sounds—"salt."

"Your mother's salt?" says Kay. "Well," she adds gently but matter-of-factly, "it'll be a lot easier to use now."

True. Or keep. Or whatever. The lump of salt is still dissolving, by now small enough to pass through the neck of the shaker. Just this morning, I was lamenting yet again the way we'd sold the sandai chest and the Chinese tapestry, without ado. No ritual of passing or farewell, no candle lit or wineglass raised to salute all they'd meant in our lives, or the people who inhabited them. Now, in mysterious synchronicity, an opportunity presents itself. Salt, that magical substance that is a vital component of life itself, the sine qua non for which the ancients traveled hundreds of miles, which the deer seek out in forests, which brings out flavors and binds moisture within its crystalline structure. My mother's salt, last touched and used by her, no one since, her essence still recorded in it, now slowly dissolving, releasing, letting go.

Almost without thinking, I dump the remains into my hand and quickly step out the kitchen door. *I'll be right back*, I say. Instinctively I go counterclockwise around the house. A bit in the herb garden, a bit on the back railing. A bit at the outside corner of the den where she and Daddy sat every night, and at the corner of their bedroom. Across the verandah where so many summer parties unfolded under Chinese lanterns, maple trees, and sunset. The boxwood bushes she loved for their stolid grace, their dark scent, their Englishness. The posts of the front porch, the doorknobs. The azaleas she planted, the nandina.

For the season, it's bitter cold, and my wet hands are freezing, the salt just a briny trace. I wipe it on the dogwood tree they planted, she and my father, and on the pillars of the Williamsburg brick carport they were so proud of. Back down the steps to the kitchen door, where my hand, just barely wet now, completes the sweep.

One family's stories are like the salt. It will last forever if you put all your attention to keeping it dry and contained. You can pour it down the drain. Or you can keep a bit of it to share, seasoning for the common pot.

Home

ACKNOWLEDGMENTS

❄

Research for *Objects of Our Affection* took me from Philadelphia to the Philippines, with many stops in between, and I am deeply indebted to the able and generous librarians, curators, scholars, and others who helped piece together the story of this family and its possessions.

Thanks to Dr. Richard Sommers of the Army War College's Military History Institute; Luther Hanson of the Army Quartermaster Museum; Dr. Gary Trogden of the U.S. Army Center of Military History; Stephen D. Coats of the Command One General Staff College Foundation; Dr. Steve Grove, retired United States Military Academy historian; Suzanne Christoff, USMA archivist, and her staff, including Alicia Muldin-Ware and Herbert LaGoy; Cols. Don Samdahl, Keith Gibson, and Diana Jacobs and Gen. James M. Morgan, ret., at Virginia Military Institute; and Dr. Brian McAllister Linn of the Texas A & M department of history.

Thanks also to Lee Arnold, director of the Historical Society of Pennsylvania library; Matthew Lyons, HSP director of archives and collections management; Carmen Valentino, appraiser for the HSP; Anna Coxe Toogood of the Independence

National Historical Park library; David Barquist of the Philadelphia Museum of Art; Ryan Semmes and the staff of the Martin Luther King Jr. Memorial Library's Washingtoniana collection; Jim Thomas of the U.S.S. *William M. Wood* Association; and Nora Graf, Sheila Stubler, Alex Wisniewski, and Dennis Lockhart at Arizona's Fort Verde Historical Museum and in the state parks system.

Thanks to all of those in Manila who helped me cover considerable territory both on the ground and in the archives, and whose hospitality and insight were unfailing: at Far Eastern University, Dr. Lourdes R. Montinola, Dr. Lydia Echauz, Dr. Elizabeth P. Melchor, Cecilia I. Anido, and Dolores S. Flora; at the Ateneo de Manila University, Fr. Jose Cruz, Dr. M. Vilches, and Milet Tendero and the staff of the American Historical Collection of the Rizal Library; at the University of the Philippines, Jose Dalisay Jr.; Serafina Joven, Myla Velasco, and the Ansett staff; guide Pablito T. Martinez; friends Jeffrey and Marga Blake; and Loline, Ken, and James Reed, who made the trip possible.

To everyone named, I cannot thank all of you enough for the hours of expertise and the generosity with which you filled in the blanks and helped excavate the history of multiple wars, the men who fought them, and the civilians who endured them.

To all the friends and colleagues from East to West who read drafts, produced clues, and patiently put up with the sometimes plodding progress of the manuscript, thanks: to Avery Rome and Ken Bookman, who read early drafts; to colleagues at the *Inquirer* who offered practical advice and moral support; to David Slavin for historical insights; to Shelly Fleming for computer expertise; to Joy Harris for insisting on that trip to Manila; and to Alexia and Mike, for a place to think. In

New Jersey, thanks to the Moorestonians—you know who you are!—and especially Berne, Judith, and the Marys; to Paul, for teaching me to go back and read the text one more time, and for that last move, with the cats in the rain, and for so much more; and to the extended South Jersey family who supported me while I was looking for the roots of my own family in Garden State soil.

To all my relations, as the Lakota prayer says: those who went before, especially Mommy, with her enduring love of history; cousins Charles III and Elizabeth; and, at the core, Jeanne and Henry (special thanks for that photo of the pistols), and David and Owen and Gabriel—you three who'll be left to sort out whatever the rest of us haven't managed. Good luck.

Objects of Our Affection would not have become a reality without my agent, Neeti Madan, who saw the possibilities inherent in an idea about how and why we hang on to things; my editor, Beth Rashbaum, whose sharp mind, keen sense of humor, gift for words, and indefatigable energy carried the book to completion; their assistants, Michelle Humphries at Sterling Lord Literistic and Angela Polidoro at Bantam, who helped make the needed connections; copy editor Emily DeHuff, who provided the finishing touches; Barbara Bachman, for her elegant design; Patti Ratchford, for a cover that sums it all up; and Charlotte, the alpha and omega, who always listened. Thank you.

Special thanks to Ginny Hillhouse for photography and conceptual design.

PHOTOGRAPHY CREDITS

...

Photographs used courtesy of the
Harlowe-Powell Auction Gallery

(IN FRONTISPIECE: George Washington chair, ladies chair,
   Empire sofa, Meissen plate, tall Korean cabinet,
   Chinese wedding lamps)
George Washington chair
Chinese wedding lamps
Sandai chest
Empire sofa
Victorian Canton vases
Hepplewhite bookcase
Cut glass master salts
Famille verte lamp

Family Photos

Harry and Nelly Egbert
Carlos with his ayah
Charles Evans Kilbourne
Bessie in her wedding gown
Bess Kilbourne and Jeanne Tracy, circa 1900
Caroline Dennis
Daniel Egbert
Charlie after World War I
The Kilbournes at VMI
Jeanne and Joe Tracy
Max Tracy, circa 1954
Sisters Jeanne, at age four, and Lisa, at age two
Betty Tracy, circa 1954

ALL OTHER PHOTOGRAPHY BY GINNY HILLHOUSE

LISA TRACY is an author and journalist and the former Home & Design editor of *The Philadelphia Inquirer*. She lives in Lexington, Virginia, where she currently teaches creative nonfiction.

This book is set in Fournier, a typeface named for Pierre Simon Fournier, the youngest son of a French printing family. Pierre Simon first studied watercolor painting, but became involved in type design through work that he did for his eldest brother. Starting with engraving woodblocks and large capitals, he later moved on to fonts of type. In 1736 he began his own foundry, and published the first version of his point system the following year. He made several important contributions in the field of type design; he cut and founded all the types himself, pioneered the concepts of the type family, and is said to have cut sixty thousand punches for 147 alphabets of his own design. He also created new printers' ornaments.